Hero's Journey
JOHN RITTER,
THE CHIP HILTON
OF GOSHEN, INDIANA

Jeff Rasley
A Memoir

COPYRIGHT 2016
JEFF RASLEY
(ALL RIGHTS RESERVED)

ISBN-13: 978-1530530182
ISBN-10: 1530530180

PUBLISHED BY
MIDSUMMER BOOKS

DEDICATION

To Clair Bee who gave us Chipper, and to John Ritter

To the friends who helped with this project; you know who you are

To Alicia for a lifetime of help

Table of Contents

Part One Expectation
Chapter One Memories of a Childhood Hero, Chip Hilton   1
Chapter Two Creation of a Childhood Hero, John Ritter   12
Chapter Three We Change, Our Heroes Change   33

Part Two Disappointment
Chapter Four Failure to Perform   43
Chapter Five Out of Step with the Culture   48
Chapter Six Estrangement from Community   54
Chapter Seven A Hero Walks a Lonely Road   67
Chapter Eight A Hero Fades from Memory   76
Chapter Nine Fallen Hero   84
Chapter Ten Rejected   94

Part Three Reconsideration
Chapter Eleven Humanity of a Hero   102
Chapter Twelve The Burden of Fame and Expectation   126
Chapter Thirteen Heroes, History, and Symbols   140

Part Four Acceptance
Chapter Fourteen Why John Ritter Ceased to Be John Ritter 154
Chapter Fifteen Rebirth   168
Chapter Sixteen The Hero's Journey Home   173
Chapter Seventeen Final Stage, Redemption from Tragic Flaw 190

Part One
Expectation

Hero: *a person who is admired or idealized for courage, outstanding achievements, or noble qualities.*
Synonyms: brave person, lionheart, warrior, knight; champion, victor, conqueror;
star, superstar, megastar, idol, celebrity, luminary; ideal, paragon, shining example, demigod; favorite, darling
Antonyms: coward, loser, unknown, nobody
The chief character in a book, play, or movie, who is typically identified with good qualities, and with whom the reader is expected to sympathize.
Synonyms: protagonist, main character, starring role
Antonyms: villain, supporting character, supporting role
(in mythology and folklore) A person of superhuman qualities and often semidivine origin, in particular one of those whose exploits and dealings with the gods were the subject of ancient Greek myths and legends.
Google Dictionary

Chapter One

Memories of a Childhood Hero, Chip Hilton

Chip Hilton was perfect - at least in my nine-year-old mind. He was tall, rangy, with blue-grey eyes and short-cropped blond hair. Chip's square jaw was always clean shaven. A lock of hair would drift down his forehead and need to be brushed back while he was playing ball.

Chip was shy around girls but popular at school with the guys. He was the star player on his high school football, basketball, and baseball teams. Chip was doted on by his hardworking, graceful and lovely mother, Mary Hilton. She always had homemade cookies ready when the guys came over after team practice.

Chip's dad, a factory foreman, died in an industrial accident saving the life of one of his crew members. Chip suffered stoically the aching loss of his father. The Hiltons were not well off, but managed. Mary worked at the factory as a secretary. Chip had to work part-time as a stock boy at the local drugstore to help with family finances.

All the good kids from the right side of the railroad tracks dividing the town liked him. Younger boys even idolized Chip because he was the best athlete in Valley Falls. But some of the tough kids from the wrong side of the tracks thought Chip was a goody-two shoes and gave him a hard time. The richest kid in town, Fats Olsen, hated Chip and was envious of his success in school and on the playing field. Fats and his henchman, Stinky Ferris, tried to sabotage Chip every chance they got.

Chip's life wasn't easy. He had school, team practices, and homework. He had to work at the drug store in the evenings and weekends. He also had chores at home, and he had to be "the man of the house".

With all these responsibilities Chip still managed to make the honor roll every semester, was the star on the Valley Falls High School teams, was a valued employee by his boss at the drug store, and never let his mom down. On and off the playing field, Chip faced up to every challenge with integrity and responsibly.

If a teammate was struggling with a personal problem, Chip was there to help. He'd give the fellow manful advice and back it up by his own example. Chip was the kind of team leader that would encourage a little horsing around during a water break in practice. But he expected the guys to be all business when Coach blew the whistle to resume drills or scrimmage.

Chip never show-boated. He'd take the blame if the team was underperforming. Once, in a football game, Chip let himself be tackled in his team's end zone, which gave the opposing team a two-point safety and made Chip look bad. It was actually a smart play, because Chip prevented a defender from recovering a fumble in the end zone which would have given the opposing team six points instead of only two. To win the game for his team, Chip was willing to look like he'd screwed up. He cared less about tarnishing his reputation in the eyes of the fans than winning the game for the team. Coach Rock and Chip's teammates understood his sacrifice.

Chip Hilton was such a straight-edged good guy. He was who I, an imaginative boy of nine wanted to be. It was the early 1960s, just before the Beatles were big. My home was in a small Midwestern town, a lot like Valley Falls. But I didn't have to face the hardships Chip did. My dad had a good job, and my mom could stay at home, so we were considerably better off than Chip and Mary Hilton. (I kind of wished my life was a little tougher, so I could be more like Chip.)

There was a not-so-subtle similarity between Chip Hilton and the Jesus I learned about in Sunday School at our Presbyterian church. Chip's mother's name was Mary. His father was in Heaven. Chip sacrificed and suffered for his team, but he always triumphed in the end. That is, by the end of the book.

Chip Hilton is the protagonist in a series of books written for boys and set in the 1950s. Clair Bee was the author. He was also the basketball coach at Long Island University.

Thankfully, Chip didn't have to die, like Jesus, to save the team. But every season in each sport, all four years of high school, things got tough and it looked like Chipper's ability to come through for the team might fail. By the end of the last chapter, Chip always figured out a way to outsmart, outwork, and overcome tough opponents, bullies at school, or financial problems at home. A sports scholarship to State University was his final reward.

Since the series sold so well, Coach Bee continued writing books about Chip as he progressed through college and was a star on the teams at State U.

Source: Amazon.com (This cover is from the revised, not original, series. The 1950s and 60s Chip Hilton that was my fictional hero was not this buff.)

-- Memory, imagination, and story --

What I've written about Chip Hilton is entirely from memory. I can recall these memories of Chip's fictional life that I have carried since childhood with what seems like perfect clarity. I have not rooted through our home library, boxes of books in the attic, or gone online to re-read any of Clair Bee's **Chip Hilton Sports Series** books. But I also know that what I remember is somewhat different than what I experienced when I read the books at ages nine and ten. There are huge gaps in my memories about specific events in the books. I have forgotten much more about what I read as a kid than what I can remember. In fact, some of the "facts" related in the preceding paragraphs about the fictional character Chip Hilton might be imagined or unintentionally invented to fill in gaps about Chip's life story. Yet, what I've written are the impressions left in my consciousness, whether or not I actually read it in Clair Bee's books.

For example, I don't remember which book it is in, but my mind "recalls" Mary Hilton being disappointed that she would be unable to attend the Company Ball for lack of a formal dress. Is that incident actually in one of the books? Details well up -- from my sub-consciousness? Mr. Olsen, the company owner, fancies Mary, but is too much the gentleman even to suggest crossing proscribed boundaries, despite his unhappy marriage to the bitchy Mrs. Olsen. He finds a way to provide Mary with the materials to fashion her own dress and appear as the beauty at the Ball. Chip and his gang chauffeured Mary in Speed Morris's souped-up convertible.

Did I make that up, or did Clair Bee? It feels so right. It might be in one of the books. Or, is it the Cinderella archetype-story surfacing from deep in my preconscious mind and polluting my memories of the Chip Hilton books. I'm not really sure.

The mind wants a complete a story to make our memories coherent. Don't you hate it when you miss the end of a show or you lose power when reading an eBook or listening to an audio-book? (I was watching the television series *Manhattan* while I was working on this book and missed the last ten minutes of the final episode. Despite efforts to procure the show through pay TV and watch the last episode, I've been unable to do so and it bugs the hell out of me!) Aristotle describes a complete literary work as simply having a beginning, middle, and end. We don't like to miss out on any one of those parts. If we do, it's unsatisfying.

There's a similar aspect to memory. We try to preserve our cherished memories in forms that have coherent meanings. We prefer our favorite memories to be complete. Dreams are often troubling because what we remember doesn't make sense and we're not sure what they mean. A bear is chasing you (is that really you, or is it someone else?). All of a sudden you're on an escalator in a large department store and you see someone you know and something else happens, but when you wake up you can't remember who the other person was for sure and what happened next. It's an inconclusive and disturbing experience. It lacks coherent meaning because the dream didn't have a beginning, middle, and end.

Disturbing dreams drift into unreachable places in our subconscious. What lingers is the feeling of disturbance. This is what dementia is like. All memories begin to fade and leave the person grasping for some bit of control.

We have a need to create and preserve meaningful and coherent memories from our past. It's unsatisfying and maddening to live with chopped up bits and chunks from our past which we can't make sense of. We want a complete narrative. So, the subconscious and conscious aspects of the mind try to fill in the gaps, to organize, and to create some kind of logic and consistency out of the scramble of data retained in our brains. A symptom of insanity is the inability to do so.

Creating and telling stories is one way humans have

dealt sanely with the random data and half-finished narratives floating in and out of their consciousness. This book is, in part, an attempt to organize and finish a story about a childhood hero from the flotsam and jetsam of memories floating around in my head.

The need to know what happened to a childhood hero and why his life went the way it did launched my search on the Internet to find information that would help create coherence and fill in blanks in my own memory. That need for a more complete story also impelled me to reach out to old friends and acquaintances of my childhood hero's to engage in conversations which would help to create a more complete characterization and narrative about him. I wanted to better understand his life journey by creating a collage of memories shared by his friends and acquaintances.

Shamans enter the dream world of sub-consciousness to wrestle with demons and rally angels. They return with tales of their encounters which become the myths and legends of their communities. The Griots of West Africa maintain and renew the oral traditions of their villages by telling the stories passed from one generation to the next. Many of the stories in the holy books of Hinduism, Buddhism, Christianity, and other religions began as oral traditions and morphed into the written versions set down by priestly scholars who wanted to rationalize the narratives of oral tradition into canonical works. The greatest bard of Hellenic civilization, Homer, wove together a patchwork of stories about Greek and Trojan heroes to create a coherent whole, **The Iliad** and **Odyssey**. Homer's Achilles, Hector, Odysseus, Aeneas, and the other legendary heroes have since populated thousands of different stories for more than a hundred generations.

Cultural archetypes are created through this process of fitting together bits of memory, visions bubbling up from the subconscious, and using imagination creatively. The process culminates in a story. Stories about an extraordinary character, whether Achilles or Chip Hilton, are the sources from which our heroes arise. A hero in a story which is compelling and meaningful can take on a life of his own which transcends the boundaries of the original story. New stories about the heroes of the ***Iliad*** have been written and produced every generation since Homer's original began circulating around the ancient Hellenic world. For me, Chip Hilton exists outside of the books in which I met him. He's no longer contained within their old worn covers.

I'm sure the same is true for many others who loved Clair Bee's books as kids. Chip became an idealized figure for his fans. He represents traditional values like courage, integrity, grit, compassion, and fidelity. His character is a model for what kids (and maybe adults) ought to be like. In that sense he is an archetypal hero for the community of the thousands who read and remember the ***Chip Hilton Sports Series***.

-- Haunted by heroes --

It's important to realize and admit that our memories are not immutable. We've all had the experience of re-telling some event with family or old friends and discovering that one of the intimate participants in the event has a different memory of what happened. Remember the game "Telephone"? A message travels around a circle of friends and by the time it gets back to the person who composed it the message has changed. "It's not exactly a comforting thought, but every time we return to the incident, we take a different route to reach it and, in turn, come home with a slightly -- or not so slightly -- different story. The mind never remembers the same way twice." (***The American Scholar***, "The Examined Lie", James McWilliams, Summer 2015, p. 20)

The classic Japanese film *Rashomon*, directed by Akira Kurosawa, makes this point more artfully. The four main characters in the film remember and re-tell the same event in four different, even contradictory, ways. Although I have the elements of the Mary Hilton at-the-Company-Ball story in my mind along with the other memorable "facts" about Chip's fictional life related above, what I actually read in the books might be slightly, significantly, or completely different. Because I have changed in the many years since I read about Chip, his mom, and his buddies in Valley Falls, my memories are different than my original encounter with those characters.

"... [M]emories are not unchanging physical traces in the brain. Instead, they are malleable constructs that may be rebuilt every time they are recalled." (**MIT Technology Review**, "Repairing Bad Memories", Stephen S. Hall, June 17, 2013, citing research by Daniela Schiller at Mount Sinai School of Medicine) Recent research by Schiller and others indicates that every time we access a memory, at the chemical level of brain function, that memory is changed if ever so slightly. In other words, our brain chemistry is changed by remembering and a memory is changed by our brain chemistry changing.

Chip Hilton has transmogrified in my consciousness from a fictional character grounded in the words Clair Bee wrote into an archetypal hero. To some extent, I've lost touch with the actuality of Chip created by the author, but my mind preserves him, changed but still accessible in flashes of images and bits of events. My mind struggles to piece together coherent narratives from these chunks of memory and imagination. But what is most clear is the impression left in my consciousness of an ideal boy, who stood for what is good and right, and how I ought to try to be like Chip.

Chip Hilton was one of my first loves, in the sense of being a devoted fan, a childish-boyhood hero worship. Maybe there was a Freudian-homoerotic element to that love. I did read the books during the pre-adolescent latency period of psychological development. But that's not my focus here, and I'm much too shy for that sort of public self-analysis. I loved Chip in a Platonic-idealistic way -- the way my Sunday School teachers wanted me to love Jesus. (Chip was definitely more fun than Jesus and his buddies much more interesting than The Disciples.)

Clair Bee's books were very entertaining to my pre-adolescent male-taste. The sports action scenes were packed with excitement; Chip throwing the game-winning pass or making the crucial basket. The characters were well developed; Speed, Biggie, Soapy, Red, and the gang were more than just cardboard characters hung around Chip's glowing star. They seemed authentic in their own right. The books were more affecting than many of the other books I read, TV shows I watched, and movies I saw. They have stayed with me because they were compelling stories which had special meaning to me during that pre-adolescent stage of development, and beyond it.

How I remember Chip fifty years later is necessarily different than my experience of reading about him when I was a kid collecting baseball cards and dreaming of being a star on the high school teams, according to current neuroscience. But the significance of Chip Hilton to those of us that have loved the books is not dependent on a perfect fit in current memory with Clair Bee's narrative. Chip affected thousands of boys (and some girls -- my wife poached a couple of the books from her brothers) growing up in the 1950s and 60s. He still has significance to many of us because he occupies space in our ever changing brain chemistry as an archetypal hero.

His affect on the community of his fans exceeds our enjoyment in bringing Chip down from "the cloud" of our memories to imagine him whacking a home run or swishing a long jump shot. We've seen and experienced tens of thousands of entertaining sports moments since we closed the last page of the last Chip Hilton book we read. Chip's effect on us goes well beyond entertainment.

Reading Clair Bee's sports books as a child was intensely emotional. My pulse quickened during the crucial moments in Chip's big games. My heart must have ached when Mary Hilton couldn't attend the Company's ball for lack of a formal dress. My fists clenched when Chip was unfairly gang-tackled. In the present, there is no intensity like that to my memories of Chip and his buddies in Valley Falls. There is a sweet and sentimental nostalgia for a time past and a culture gone with the wind.

The lingering effect is that I am indebted to, and in a way cursed by, Chip Hilton. (I suppose, more accurately, it is Clair Bee, Chip's creator, I should credit and blame.) As Chip developed in my consciousness as the ideal of what I thought a boy ought to be like, he also became an inspiration, to be like Chip. But my dream, as for most of Chip's fans, of following in his footsteps to glory on high school and college sports teams eventually died at some point during adolescence. Since then, Chip has sat in lofty judgment of my failings. He haunts me, because I will never be as good, on or off the field, as Chip Hilton.

Of course, Chip Hilton could not be my hero after childhood passed away. And now, I am much older than he will ever be. Yet, there is a ghostly aspect to my memories of Chip. He doesn't stir passions as he did in my nine year-old self. He can fade in and out of my consciousness like a dream, changing uniforms, ethereal, but forever young. He haunts me for who I did not become. Because there is still the vestige of that nine year-old self which wants to be like Chip within me. That is an unanticipated consequence of childish hero worship.

Our heroes inspire us. But the vast vast majority of us will not live up to the expectations we develop for ourselves by idealizing them.

Flesh and blood heroes pose an even greater risk, and not just to their fans. They might threaten to haunt us for our failures to live up to their heroic ideals, but they also risk failing to live up to our expectations.

Chapter Two

Creation of a Childhood Hero, John Ritter

John Ritter was a real-live Chip Hilton in my home town, Goshen, Indiana. I also met him when I was nine-years old. And, the memory of what John Ritter was like as a high school sports star still haunts me.

I've spoken with many people who knew John Ritter when he was the golden boy of our hometown. When we talk about him now, so many decades after his heroics on our playing fields, John Ritter still stirs up our emotions. A door is opened to memories locked away in the attic and ghosts come flitting out. As one old friend of John's said to me, "It brings tears to my eyes, when I think of what's happened to him."

I'd over-heard snatches of adult conversations at the Rexall Drug Store in downtown Goshen about this older kid named John Ritter. He was supposed to be a sports phenomenon like we'd never had before in a boy from Goshen. Before he finished junior high school he could beat high school players one-on-one in basketball. He could throw a football or baseball with pinpoint accuracy.

My first experience of organized athletics was summer-league baseball sponsored by the Fraternal Order of Police for eight and nine year-old boys. John Ritter had a summer job helping Mr. Phend run the FOP baseball program. John was the home-plate umpire when I played the best game of my young life. I pitched a winning game for our normally pretty-miserable Pirates team. I got a hit every time I came up to bat, including a home run and a couple doubles. After the game John slapped me on the back and said, "Great game, Rasley!" And then something about keep working on my pitching and he expected "great things" from me.

I was in Seventh Heaven. I'd been praised by John Ritter! This was the kid the grown-ups talked about over coffee and Cokes. John Ritter was our hope for the future, the athlete who would put our town on the map for what we most cherished -- a basketball championship for the Goshen High School Redskins. He had praised me!

When I got home after that game I drew a strike zone on a wall in our basement. I threw a rubber baseball against that wall until my arm was worn out.

It happened. John Ritter fulfilled our expectations. He became a record-breaking high school basketball player and star pitcher on the baseball team. He probably would have been the star of the football team too, just like Chip. But, by the late 1960s basketball coaches had begun to discourage their best players from playing football out of concern for injuries and missed playing time.

Ritter's talent and grit on the high school basketball team so far exceeded that of his teammates that he could play every position. He could jump the highest, so he jumped center for tip offs. He could dribble and pass better than the other guards on the team, so he sometimes played the point to bring the ball down court. He was the best rebounder and excellent defender, so John was usually assigned the best player on the opposing team to guard. The Redskins' offense ran through John and was designed to give him open shots, because he was a dead-eye shooter, or for him to pass to an open teammate when the opponents double-teamed him.

John Ritter graduated from high school in 1969, but his name is still at the top of the Goshen High School Basketball record book in every scoring category. Even though John played before the 3-point shot rule, he still has the record for most points scored in a career at 1,523, over 200 points higher than second place;, most points in a season at 769, almost 200 points higher than second. John's name is also in third place for his junior year at 509 points, which is the record for most points scored by a junior. He scored the most points in a single game with 49; nine points higher than second place. John shares the record for most rebounds in a game. He won the Northern Conference scoring title with a 29.6 point average and set a new record for points scored in a career for Elkhart County high school players. He was the first, and is still one of only two, Goshen Redskins ever chosen to be an Indiana High School All-Star. The only Goshen boys' basketball team in the history of the school to win the regional tournament and reach the "Semi-State" was the 1968-69 team captained by John Ritter.

The legendary UCLA basketball coach John Wooden came to our little town to recruit Ritter. A photograph of a smiling Wooden leaning toward the photographer was published in the *Goshen News*.

Art Cosgrove, John's high school coach, is slouched in between Wooden and John smiling slyly. John's right hand is wrapped from an injury he sustained playing baseball.

Although the photo was taken in 1969, John is the picture of a conservative youthful-athlete from the 1950s and early 60s before the Beatles were big. His could be the image chosen by Clair Bee for a ***Chip Hilton Sports Series*** book.

According to the accompanying ***Goshen News*** article, John Ritter was considered such a valuable addition to a college basketball program he was recruited by over 200 schools. But the talk of the town, when sports guys gathered, was whether Ritter should choose IU or UCLA.

John Wooden was very popular in Indiana. He was the star of his high school team in the small town of Martinsville and led the team to a state championship. At Purdue University Wooden was a three-time All-American. Wooden's coaching career began at South Bend Central High School, where his teams played against the Goshen Redskins several times. His first college job was coaching at Indiana State University. Wooden's teams played against teams coached by Art Cosgrove, who was the St. Joseph's College coach for several years before coming to Goshen. Wooden probably expected his old foe Cosgrove to be an ally in persuading Ritter to choose UCLA over IU.

Coach Wooden failed in his attempt to lure John out to Los Angeles to play for the Bruins. A loyal Hoosier, Ritter accepted a scholarship to his home-state university (just like Chip Hilton). John became a star forward/guard at Indiana University.

John Ritter

Source: Indiana University Athletic Dept.

Like Chip, John Ritter was tall, six foot five, and rangy with neatly trimmed light-brown hair and blue eyes. He was always clean-shaven. John was a couple inches taller than Chip, but star basketball players were generally taller in the 1960s-70s than in the 40s and 50s.

John was also a good guy like Chip Hilton. He walked through the halls of Goshen High School with an easy confidence, but he was not thought of as stuck up by the other kids. He was actually a little shy, especially around girls, but had a ready smile and handshake or pat on the back for anyone who needed it. John was intensely focused when playing ball, but off the court he was mild tempered. John was a good Joe and a straight shooter.

John was from a modest background, like Chip. But John's father was not deceased. In fact, he came to the gym and sat through the high school team's practices intently watching his son. John's parents went to all the home and away games proudly watching their son's triumphs on the basketball court and baseball diamond. John was the middle of three brothers.

Mr. Ritter had worked as a bus driver but spent most of his career with the local power company, Northern Indiana Public Service Company (NIPSCO). He walked with a pronounced limp, and I think he might have ended up on disability from NIPSCO. (My recollection does not include a story that John's dad was injured while saving the life of a co-worker.) Mrs. Ritter, like Mary Hilton, worked at a local factory in the shipping department.

John Ritter was our chosen one. The whole town of Goshen took pride in our favorite son. In the winter of 1969, when the basketball team came back after winning the high school regional tournament but losing the semi-state game, a crowd of cheering supporters waited at the high school parking lot to greet John and his teammates. They hadn't won the championship, but they drew statewide attention to our town. Our boys had played well, and John Ritter was selected for the Indiana All-Stars Team; the first Goshen player to be so honored. Not bad for a small-town team going up against big schools from Gary, South Bend, Ft. Wayne, and Indianapolis. (Indiana's high school basketball tournament did not segregate teams into classes based on school size until 1998.)

-- *The best white player* --

John's image shooting a jump shot was used on posters

to promote the Indiana High School Athletic Association's (IHSAA) statewide boys tournament for the 1968-69 season. (There was no girls tournament, because there were no IHSAA-sanctioned girls teams in the pre Title IX era.) Goshen didn't win the state championship and John was not chosen as Indiana's "Mr. Basketball" (the recognition awarded by the *Indianapolis Star* and conferred on the best player of the crop of graduating high school seniors by the IHSAA). The terrifically talented George McGinnis of Washington High School, a predominantly African-American school located in the inner-city of Indianapolis, was named Mr. Basketball for the Class of 1969.

High school basketball in Indiana had opened up to black kids in the 1950s and teams with outstanding African-American players often won state titles. In 1955 Crispus Attucks High School won the state championship. According to *Wikipedia*, it was the first all-black team to win a state championship in the entire country, and it was the first Indiana high school team that had an undefeated season along with winning the title game. The Big O, Oscar Robertson, was the star of the Tigers 1955 team. (The smallest school ever to win the state championship, "the mighty men of Milan", on which the movie *Hoosiers* is based, took the title the previous year in 1954.)

The 1968-69 Indiana high school basketball season had another undefeated championship team, which was McGinnis's Washington High Continentals. Big George was nick-named "The Baby Bull" and "Big Mac", because he was such an imposing force on the basketball court. McGinnis's teammate, Steve Downing, was also a towering presence and outstanding player. Both of these eighteen-year-olds stood six foot eight and weighed around 230 pounds. With McGinnis and Downing as running mates the Continentals blasted through the state tournament until they met another predominantly African-American team in the final game. But Washington prevailed over Gary Tolleson 79-76. McGinnis scored 35 points; Downing added 20.

Despite that George McGinnis was Mr. Basketball, it was John Ritter's small-town white-boy image taped to windows and walls in downtown stores, barber shops, and bars in towns all across Northern Indiana on the poster with the schedule for the 1969 state tournament. Goshen was thrilled to see our high school hero as the face of Indiana high school basketball. (Not sure that sentiment was shared by McGinnis, Downing, or the fans of the Washington Continentals.)

John's Chip Hilton-like image might have been preferred to that of the imposing bruiser McGinnis as representative of "Hoosier Hysteria" around Goshen. But the alumni boosters of Indiana University basketball were thrilled that McGinnis, Steve Downing, and John Ritter had each agreed to enroll at IU as freshmen in the Fall of 1969. The future of Hoosier basketball rested on the broad and capable shoulders of these three Indiana High School All-Stars. Expectations were sky high, but Hoosier fans would have to wait patiently through another basketball season. Freshmen were not allowed to play varsity basketball under National Collegiate Athletic Association (NCAA) rules in 1969.

-- *Community roots* --

Goshen's "metro" population was around 13,000, when John and I were growing up in the 1950s-60s. There was a population surge during the late 60s into the 70s, largely due to migrations of poor white folks from Appalachia applying for jobs in the booming mobile home and recreational vehicle (RV) industries. RV factories began popping up in Elkhart County in the 1960s. The Goshen area became "the capitol of the RV industry" as local entrepreneurs jumped on the opportunity created by the growing demand of middle-class Americans to travel their country in self-contained luxury.

A second even greater population increase began in the

1980s, and really boosted the town's numbers in the 1990s, by mostly Hispanics to fill low end jobs in the once-again booming RV industry. Goshen's population topped 31,000 in 2010. (*Stats/Indiana*, Goshen population entry)

    Goshen had a stable and diversified economy during the childhoods of the post-war baby boomers. There were several small factories around town and many successful family farms in the townships outside of town. The heroin shot in the arm for the local economy from the RV industry and consequent population surges from "outsiders" began about the time John entered high school. Before that, class enrollments in the township schools were as low as ten students in the 1950s and early 60s.

    The Ritters' home was outside of town in rural Elkhart Township, so John attended township schools until he entered Goshen High School as a freshman. The graduating class of Goshen High for 1969, pumped up by Baby Boomers and the children of the "Appalachian migration", was the largest ever; 264 by count of the seniors pictured and listed in the Crimson, the GHS yearbook for John's class of 1969.

    John and I grew up in a time when families left town for winter vacations in Florida or a summer weekend at Lake Wawasee without feeling the need to lock their doors. Neighbors knew each other, perhaps too well, and adults did not hesitate to comment or intervene when children misbehaved. The town was proud of its schools, especially Goshen High. The sports teams, as well as band, orchestra, and choir were well-funded and the focus of much attention and concern within the community.

    For middle-class kids in Goshen, life in the 1950s and early 60s was pretty much like the postcard picture of small-town America. There were many white picket fences around town. Dads went to work and brought home the bacon. Most of the moms stayed home and took care of the kids. Girls played with their Barbie Dolls. Boys and tomboys played sports, fished, and caught crawdads along the banks of the

Elkhart River. We saw ourselves and our way of life portrayed in TV shows, like *Leave it to Beaver, Father Knows Best*, and *My Three Sons*. We were, as yet, undisturbed by the mounting discontent over the war in Viet Nam and charged racial issues impacting urban life in the US.

We didn't have a caste system per se, but there was not a lot of social or economic mobility. It was expected that children of the middle class would "do better" than their parents. Exceptional kids in the working class were afforded the same latitude in opportunity. But, as my high school Civics Class teacher put it, "There are Indians and Chiefs. Not everybody gets to be a Chief." Folks tended to know their place.

The poorest families lived in a little shanty row along Olive Street on the northeast side. Most of the blue-collar working-class families lived north of the railroad tracks which divided the town. White collar folks and prosperous merchants tended to live south of the tracks. Farm kids and "suburbanites" living outside the city limits in Elkhart Township were bussed in to Goshen High.

John, like most township kids, integrated into the established social circles of the south-side-of-the-tracks kids in high school. The family didn't qualify for the inner-circle of Goshen society, such as it was, but John was considered one of the "good kids". He dressed, groomed, and behaved correctly, according to the expectations set for the sons and daughters of the merchant and professional class on the "right side" of the tracks.

In fact, John Ritter was a better kid than us south-siders whose families thought of themselves as the social elite of Goshen. He had Chip Hilton-like good looks. He was the best athlete in town. He was very bright; an A-student. John was placed into the two "advanced classes" offered in our school system, Math and English. (Advanced classes were the 1960s version of Advanced Placement courses.) He made National Honor Society junior year and reportedly earned the highest score of his class on the SAT. John was popular with his peers. He was elected vice-president of Student Government and chosen to be co-captain of the high school baseball and basketball teams.

John Ritter was a straight shooter on and off the court. He was the kind of kid who'd politely answer grown-ups with, "Yes, ma'am" and "No, sir". He was certainly big enough that he could have been a bully; as many of the bigger boys were during a time before the current sensitivity to bullying. John was just the opposite. He didn't have a mean bone in his body. He was deferential to adults, shy around girls, and a "hail fellow well met" around guys. His baseball coach from freshman through senior year said of John, "He didn't have any vices. He just seemed to be as pure as he could be."

John must have known he was "better" than the rest of us in so many ways. But he didn't show it. He seemed sincerely humble.

In the 1960s, after President Kennedy declared that we would beat the Soviets to the Moon by the end of the decade, US astronauts became the coolest guys on the planet to patriotic Americans. The race was won the summer John Ritter graduated from high school in 1969, when Neil Armstrong took his giant step and planted the Stars and Stripes on the Moon. The "can do" optimistic attitude, conservative All-American look, and understated competence of our astronaut heroes (portrayed really well in the 1983 movie based on the Tom Wolfe novel, *The Right Stuff*, as well as the 1995 movie *Apollo 13*, and more recently the book and movie, *The Martian*) -- if any kid growing up in Goshen, Indiana, during that era had the right stuff, it was John Ritter. In this younger boy's eyes, he was about as perfect as a boy could be.

-- Digression on Goshen cred --

Here, I feel the need to present my credentials to claim

a limited right to speak for Goshen, Indiana, it's local culture, and the character of the town while John Ritter and I were boys growing up in the post-war baby boom.

Ancestors on my mother's side of the family were early pioneer settlers in the Goshen area. My great-great grandfather, with the endearing name of Valentine Berkey, owned a farm with a large swath of land that became the west side of Goshen. The street running alongside where the farmhouse still stands is named Berkey Avenue. The house was conserved by local historical preservationists and is now owned by the West Goshen Church of the Brethren.

My ancestors have been integrally involved with the community in business, politics, and culture. My mother's grandfather, Jesse Heefner, was a local fishing guide, owned a general store on Main Street, and served as truant officer for the town schools. His wife, Ella Mae Heefner, was a teacher when Goshen had a one-room schoolhouse and then served as truant officer after Jesse's death. My mom's father, Joe Stutz, was a high school football and basketball star and player-coach on the local semi-pro football team, the Goshen Grays, in the 1920s. Two generations of my family edited the local newspaper, *Goshen News*, and my mother and step-father wrote *Goshen: the First 150 Years Goshen, Indiana Sesquicentennial Edition 1831-1981* for the Goshen Historical Society. My father was the personnel director for Reith-Riley Construction Co., one of the largest employers in northern Indiana. My brother served a term as a city councilman. Great grandparents, grandparents, and parents served as deacons and elders in the First Presbyterian Church of Goshen. On Sundays, when I was a child, four generations of my family sat in "our pew".

I mention my local ancestry in order to explain how deeply rooted in Goshen I felt as a child growing up within the community. My family was not rich or powerful, but we were involved. Our identity was thoroughly intertwined with that of the town.

No one in my family lives in Goshen any longer. The chain has been broken. I haven't lived there since 1975, but I think distance has given me a better perspective to speak for the town the way it was.

Because of my intimacy and distance I can hear the voice of Goshen talking about John Ritter like a Greek Chorus. It was loud and raucous when cheering his high school and college triumphs. It faded as he left the public stage. But it still mutters with curiosity about what happened to our golden boy.

-- *Relative perspective* --

I must also admit that the memories shared in this book about John and our hometown, like those about Chip Hilton, may be subject to question. A popular trope in current literary fiction is the "unreliable narrator". (It's actually an ancient technique used as long ago as the early 17th Century by Miguel de Cervantes in **Don Quixote**.) Nonfiction works, particularly biographies and memoirs, are expected by traditional definition to be factually reliable. Choosing not to re-read the Chip Hilton books and track down the questionable "facts" about Chip's story may be considered a violation of standards for a work of nonfiction (or laziness). The words Clair Bee wrote have not changed, so the truth is there between the covers to confirm or contradict my memories.

Except, in a way, the words have changed. In the late 1990s the series was re-issued by a different publisher at the behest of Bee's children. The new publisher is a "Christian" organization and it has revised the narratives and language to reflect an "evangelical flavor", according to Thomas M. DeFrank in "Sporting Legend Returns", **Daily News**, August 4, 2002.

Still, I could have purchased the original series of Chip Hilton books on eBay, and then re-read all of them to fact-check against my memories. But the specific "facts" are not what is vital for the purposes of *this* book. What's essential is the meaning Chip represents for me and other kids of the Baby Boom generation and what he can mean for you through this book.

John Ritter's story, on the other hand, is about a real person, and so one might think it should be diligently fact-checked for the truth. But is that expectation actually realistic? The response provided by Kurosowa's *Rashomon* is a resounding, No!

John Ritter will have different memories than I do, and we will both remember and interpret events different than other sources. I encountered several conflicting recollections of very specific events talking to old friends and acquaintances from Goshen about John. For example, I've spoken with several members of the high school baseball team, and the head coach, about a couple incidents involving the team when John was a senior and co-captain of the team. Each of these sources has a different memory and different interpretation of the events.

A personal example of the "truthiness" of memory is my recollection of our "G-Mens Banquet" John's senior year. I "clearly" remembered that John Wooden was the speaker, and even recalled him joking with and about John during the talk. My friend "Mel", who also attended the banquet, disputed my recollection. He insisted the speaker was Coach Tony Hinkle of Butler University. The day after our conversation he emailed me to report we were both wrong, the speaker was Lou Watson from Indiana University. I felt compelled to track down "the truth" through a search of **Goshen News** articles. Confronted with a print record my memory cleared somewhat as I relate later in the book.

Trial lawyers are well aware of the shortcomings of relying on accounts of eye witnesses. Many an innocent defendant has gone to the gallows based on what was later proved to be the inaccurate memory of eye witness testimony.

I'm not an intentionally unreliable narrator. Neither am I an omniscient narrator. I recognize that others with a different perspective might disagree with some of my interpretations, theories, and guess-work about John Ritter's story. I have included in the narrative instances of conflicting recollections of "witnesses". In other cases, to create a coherent story, I report what resonates most strongly with my own understanding. I have researched all "free" sources on the Internet to resolve any factual discrepancies that might be clarified (like, who was the speaker at the 1969 Goshen High sports banquet), but I have not spent the time to poke through dusty archives or paid subscription fees to access all possible digital records. The result is not a strictly linear account but a collage of historical accounts from articles and memories of people who have known John Ritter at various stages of his life.

Declarative statements about John and descriptions of particular events are sourced. When I propose a hypothesis to fill in a gap for lack of complete information, or posit a theory or opinion, those instances should be clear in the text. I do report rumors as rumors received through the "Goshen grapevine" that I recall and have been mentioned by at least one other person. I did not formally interview any of the "witnesses" who appear in later chapters. The reminiscences about John Ritter that they shared were in conversations about a person of mutual interest that we admire and care about. There might even be discrepancies between my friends' memories and mine of our conversations, but this is my memoir. These friendly sources were aware I was writing about John and they knew I might quote them. For the sake of personal privacy, I do not name, or I change the name, of John's contemporaries who are sources.

No piece of writing perfectly duplicates memory, let alone the reality of another person. But words are the only tools I have to work with to tell my story about Chipper and Ritter, what they have meant to me, and what it means to be a hero.

[John Ritter was not interviewed for this book. In deference to his implied request, I did not speak with his siblings or his children. The reader's curiosity will be satisfied in Chapter Ten where it is explained why John chose not to be interviewed. I just want to note here that I have not tried to search out and discover whatever it is that John did not want his family to read about, and I did not contact members of his family. But I do include in my story what friendly "witnesses" told me they know or remember about troubled times in John's life journey.]

What is most important to me as the author is that the meanings offered by Chip Hilton's and John Ritter's stories are clearly expressed. That is why I am introducing you to these two characters. I do not claim to know and to be telling The Truth about Chip or John. They have both slipped out of the realm of experiential fact to become more like archetypes in my mind. As you read on, you'll understand that John means more than that to me, because he is real and has feelings and his own life and concerns. He is a fellow human being. But he also exists, like Chip, as representative of more than the memorable experiences he gave to his fans.

John's extraordinary gifts, his unique personality, and the way his life developed lift him up to be wondered at by those of us who encountered him and know at least part of his story. So, despite the fallibility of memory and the inability ever to discover and relate the whole truth about real (or fictional) heroes, my hope is that through telling John Ritter's story, as I know it, we will learn something worthwhile about how we create, treat, and mistreat our heroes; how they can let us down, and why we still need them.

-- Divergence of expectation and reality --

Before he narrowed his choices down to IU and UCLA, John made campus visits to several other schools that tried to woo him with scholarship offers. John told a teammate on the high school baseball team that two different schools offered him bribes and favors. John sensed that another program wanted him on the team specifically because he was white. He concluded that the school had unwritten racist recruiting practices.

John removed each of these programs from his list of possible choices for college, because he wanted nothing to do with an athletic program that was morally tainted. John told his teammate that what he was promised by the coaching staff at IU was "the opportunity to play if you work your butt off." That was the ethic John was looking for, his buddy told me.

So, what was it like for John Ritter, who grew up in a rural area to matriculate at a university that had twice as many students as the entire population of Goshen? What was it like for a boy from a lily-white town to play on a team and in a sport that was becoming dominated by African-Americans from densely populated urban areas? New challenges for Goshen's golden boy awaited him at Indiana University.

Growing up in Goshen in the 1950s and 60s, we were never around African-Americans, except when we played against black kids on opposing teams from South Bend, Elkhart, and Ft. Wayne. In school, church, and home we were properly instructed not to be racist and that the N-word was prohibited same as the F-word. We just didn't have much of an opportunity to be tested on our racial sensitivity.

When my 7th grade football team was suiting up to play a predominantly African-American school's team in Elkhart, our coach felt the need to buck up our confidence with this advice: "Don't worry fellas, those black kids put their pants on just like you do, one leg at a time." (We discovered, however, that their legs were much stronger than ours as they proceeded to beat the crap out of us, 36-0.)

Future NBA legend Larry Bird followed in John Ritter's footsteps to IU. He was five years younger and four inches taller, but also from a small Hoosier town and played ball with a style very similar to Ritter's. (John actually scouted Bird unofficially and recommended him to Coach Bob Knight after John's graduation from IU.) When Bird entered IU he was a ballyhooed white kid from a small town that could do it all on the court. But Bird quit school before he played a game for the Hoosiers. Larry recognized that he needed more time to mature as a person and to deal with issues at home before he was ready for college. His success at the much smaller and closer-to-home Indiana State University in Terre Haute set the table for Bird to become Larry Legend.

John's life might have taken a different route if he too had stayed closer to home and chosen a smaller school with a less challenging culture than IU. Perhaps John could have done for Ball State, for instance, what Bird did for Indiana State. Alternatively, had he accepted Coach Wooden's offer, John would have been on NCAA championship teams every year, and he would have been mentored by the finest gentleman in college basketball. Playing on teams that won consecutive national championships under John Wooden would surely have altered John's life from the course it took playing at IU under the volatile Bobby Knight. But the die was cast.

I didn't know much about what John's life was actually like at IU, while I was still in high school. No rumors of problems or friction with the coaching staff surfaced in Goshen that I was aware of. John Ritter put our town on the map and made us proud that one of our own was living the dream of every small town boy who shot baskets at a hoop nailed to the garage or barn. That's my recollection of what I thought at the time, anyway.

From talking with John's freshman college roommate, Tad (I've changed his name), I learned that John was popular in the "jocks' dorm" in McNutt Quad. But John wasn't really intimately friendly with any of the guys. As in high school, he was popular as a role model, who did everything "the right way". John worked very hard at academics, and was particularly serious about courses in his Business-Finance major. Tad said, "John was disappointed if he got a 3.8, that's how serious he was about school." But Tad quickly added, "John wasn't a drudge. He had a great sense of humor."

A couple other teammates of John's in high school, who met up with him a few times at IU passed on a "story" they'd heard about John being rushed by a fraternity. John supposedly asked whether there was any drinking at the House. The response was something like, "Uh, it's a college fraternity, what do you think?" John chose not to join.

In Ritter's senior year IU made it to the NCAA Final Four. As fickle fate would have it, the Hoosiers faced John Wooden's UCLA Bruins led by Bill Walton. "Good Luck" signs supporting Ritter and the Hoosiers were taped to windows on houses and stores all over Goshen. John is quoted in a story by sports reporter Stu Swartz for the *Goshen News*: "I received a telegram from Goshen ... There were so many names on it, they had to use two envelopes."

Before the game commenced, John's can-do attitude and Hoosier loyalty is encapsulated in this quote from an interview: "This is a combination of everything I have done in my playing days. For us to be here is equivalent of being in the state high school finals. Coach Knight said at the start of the season that this is where we want to be while other teams are in mothballs. When I went to Bloomington, I wanted to help put IU basketball back on top." (*Hoosier Morning*, Posted by Hugh Kellenberger, comment by The New Coke, Nov. 4, 2009)

Until Goshen High was knocked out of the tournament John's senior year, he'd had about as much experience with failure as he'd had with African-Americans; not much. But Goshen didn't win the IHSAA Tournament John's senior year in high school. And IU didn't win the NCAA Tournament John's senior year in college. In high school and college John's teams fell just short of the ultimate prize, a championship trophy. In Chip Hilton's idealized-fictional world, Valley Falls High School and State University, led by Chip, always managed to pull off the final big win needed to capture a league title or championship by the end of the book.

After IU's loss to UCLA in the 1973 NCAA semifinals, the Hoosiers whipped Providence in the consolation match 97-79. In his final game as a college player, Ritter scored 21 points and grabbed seven rebounds -- a triumphant finish, if not a championship -- to end his basketball career at Indiana University. But there was a nuance, a crack in the exterior of Chipper-like perfection, evidenced in a post-game interview John gave which was quoted in that *Goshen News* article by Stu Swartz: "It's kind of a feeling of relief ... There was a lot of pressure I won't have to worry about any more ..."

John was an Academic All-American, so his interviews were likely more articulate than the string of sports clichés we're used to hearing muttered or bellowed into a microphone by college athletes. But that last interview was remarkably introspective; "... a feeling of relief ... a lot of pressure ... I won't have to worry about any more ..."

There may have been earlier hints that John did not feel perfect or perfectly at peace with himself. But John's statement about his need for relief from the pressure he felt made it pretty clear that he was not completely happy with how things had worked out for him at IU under Coach Knight.

It took about twenty-seven years before John found the release he needed.

Chip Hilton's post-game commentaries were always marked with humility and credit given to other players and the coaches. But Chip always has the next season to look forward to. His life as a sports hero never ends. His fans can reread the series after they finish the last book. Even after the last book about Chip is closed for the last time, he lives on in our collective memory. Chip can replay his triumphant moments on the court, diamond, and field forever without end.

Not so for John Ritter. He might have lived on in the collective memory of his Goshen and IU fans as our Chip Hilton-like hero, if his life had gone the way his fans expected it would. But John is not a fictional character. Real life does not necessarily go the way we want it to for ourselves or for our heroes. His went down an unexpected path that radically changes John Ritter's image as an archetypal hero from his alter-ego, Chip Hilton.

Chapter Three
We Change, Our Heroes Change

Choosing a hero is a delicate business, one that shouldn't be undertaken frivolously. For the heroes that we choose, whether real or imagined, from the world of fact or the pages of fiction, will determine to a greater or lesser degree the things that we do and ultimately, if we allow them the privilege, the lives we will lead. From the Canadian story-teller Stuart McLean's monologue in *Vinyl Cafe*, February 21, 2016, "Stamps".

McLean's story is about two boys, Sam and Murphy, "swinging in the awkward playground in between (they are pre-adolescents) ... old enough to recognize a heroic feat when they see one and young enough to answer the call of who knows what trumpet should it stir them to action." The boys learn about the greatest of all philatelists (stamp collectors), Philipp von Ferrary, and they are inspired to go on a quest to find the most valuable of all stamps. They find instead, beauty, the value of hard work, and a deeper understanding of responsibility. The story ends with the narrator explaining that von Ferrary "is no longer a hero, but a comrade in arms." By that, McLean meant that they had come to understand what really motivated and inspired von Ferrary, and it wasn't the material value of the stamp. The boys learned that living according to the ideals they discovered has more value than the most expensive stamp in the world. Their quest became a first step on their own Hero's Journey.

After my little league encounter with John Ritter my personal contact with him was minimal. We went to different elementary schools. There were two junior high schools that fed into Goshen High School. Since John lived outside the city boundary, he attended Elkhart Township Junior High. I lived just inside the city, so I went to Goshen Junior High. John was a senior, when I entered high school. I admired my hero from afar; which, in a small town with one high school, was not all that far.

Still, I didn't have the chutzpah in high school to remind John of our encounter in little league baseball. He was too far above me in the high school pecking order of social status to buttonhole him in the hallway for either a casual or serious conversation. Anyway, what could I have said that wouldn't have come off sounding pathetic and lame? "Gee whilikers, Mr. Superstar of our high school, remember when ..." Uh, not cool.

Like most boys in Goshen with less than stellar athletic abilities, my childhood dreams of stardom on the basketball and football teams crashed on the rocky shoals of reality by the time I was in high school. I ran track, swam, and played summer-league baseball after having tired of sitting on the bench as a third-stringer on the basketball team. I quit football after deciding there were many more enjoyable ways to spend the last two weeks of summer vacation than sweating through two-a-day practices in the heat and humidity of August.

All of us less gifted and less committed jocks, as well as the guys in the Boys Booster Club, the cheerleaders, Girls Cheer Block, and adult supporters of our high school sports teams, recognized John Ritter as a very special basketball player. There were other very good athletes around town and guys that had been stars for the Redskins in the past, but Ritter was going to lead our basketball team, who knows, maybe all the way to a state championship. We felt lucky and grateful to be Redskins fans during the John Ritter era.

There's a 1986 coming of age movie, *Lucas* (young Charlie Sheen and Winona Rider have co-starring roles), set within the society of a small town high school. The guys on the football team are big and strong and look so tough in their uniforms. The cheerleaders are the cutest girls in school. That's how the school's jocks and cheerleaders are seen by the rest of the kids anyway. The movie is a dramatic illustration of relative perspective. When the local boys go up against a big city school, the locals no longer look so impressive. The other team's uniforms are more colorful, much sharper and stylish. Their players are bigger, stronger, and faster. The cheerleaders from the big urban school are much hotter and their cheer routines are really sexy. The outfits of the home team cheerleaders look frumpy and old-fashioned in comparison, and the cheers sound uninspiring and lame.

It wasn't that bad, but Goshen fans could certainly relate to the theme of small town inferiority complex. We rarely won when our teams played the big schools from South Bend and Fort Wayne. Worst of all was Elkhart High School, which we thought of as our biggest rival. Goshen lost to Elkhart in basketball 38 consecutive times in one stretch. It was just as bad, if not worse, in football. The Redskins basketball record against the Blue Blazers was 43 wins and 95 losses until Elkhart High was split into two schools in 1972.

But, oh man! When John Ritter played for the Redskins, we beat the Blue Blazers twice John's sophomore year, and most significantly, in the sectional tournament his senior year. He was the one player we had that could out shine anybody from the big schools in all of Northern Indiana.

John Ritter's impact on sports lovers in the Goshen area can't be exactly quantified, but as an imperfect measure of it, there are over fifty references to his name in archived *Goshen News* articles just since 2013. That's as far back as the digitized archives go. These articles are mostly "Remember When" sorts of pieces about particularly outstanding performances by John on his high school and college teams. If a researcher could count every mention of John Ritter on sports pages in northern Indiana, beginning with Ritter's freshman year on the high school basketball and baseball teams through all the reminiscences about him, the number of entries would be astronomical.

Recognition of John's excellence in athletics, academics, and character continued through his graduation at IU. In addition to being named an academic All-American and selected for the second team of Big Ten All-Stars, John was a two-time winner of the Balfour Award "for bringing honor and distinction" to IU, and received the Jake Gimbel Award for "excellence in athletics and scholarship and outstanding mental attitude". He was chosen to be the Honorary Parade Marshall of the 1973 Putnam County 4-H Fair Parade. The *Banner Graphic* of Greencastle, Indiana, in a page 1 article about John's selection as Parade Marshall, stated, "His basketball and academic achievements emphasize this year's theme of service to America."

From the perspective of a kid two grades behind him and five inches shorter, it looked like John's popularity and achievements came naturally and easily to him. Not that he didn't work hard. To the contrary, John Ritter's fans loved the way he combined grit and finesse on the court. He gave everything he attempted that one hundred ten percent (in the annoying phraseology of coaches) required of winners. It's just that his excellence always looked effortless in comparison to the rest of us kids grunting and sweating in his wake.

But John was not full of himself. On the contrary, like Chip Hilton, he seemed sincerely humble, kind, and thoughtful of others. A high school baseball teammate of John's put it this way: "John was almost too good to be true. He didn't smoke, drink or cuss. I never heard him raise his voice in anger, only enthusiastic encouragement for our teammates."

A high school classmate of John's described him as "graceful in the way he played ball and the way he conducted himself." Another high school contemporary told me that John was even "the star in Typing Class".

Jeez! Did he have to be the best in everything, even typing?! Couldn't he at least be a humorless robot!? Nope;

Ritter's chums admired John for his quick wit and clever sense of humor in the locker room. Several older acquaintances of mine, who knew John while they were growing up in Goshen, related that he had "a great sense of humor". John Ritter seemed to exist in a rarefied atmosphere that only he breathed.

But there was something else about John, other than his talents and achievements, that separated him from his peers. A classmate of John's, with whom I recently reconnected through Facebook, told me that very few kids actually got to know John well. John was, indeed, "a natural leader within the Class of 69, always courteous and friendly to everyone, yet sort of stand-offish", my friend said. He was "somehow one of the guys, yet not really a part of regular society within our Class."

The word a friend and teammate of John's, who was a year ahead of John in school, used to describe the way John related to friends and guys on his teams was "cordial". "Sam" and John were on an undefeated little league baseball team together. They began playing basketball with and against each other when Sam was in eighth grade and John in seventh at Elkhart Township Junior High. Sam played on the high school team with John, until he quit junior year. Sam also attended IU, ran into John on campus occasionally, and played pickup ball with him in Goshen at Rogers Park during summer breaks. So, Sam had been a friend of John's and was around him on a regular basis from early adolescence through college.

He related to me that John never cussed, drank, smoked, or misbehaved in any way. "He was a good sport, played hard, and never said a bad word. John never missed practice or a game." Still, there was a distance between John and his teammates. "We'd go to the Soda Shop and horse around after a game, but John never hung out with the team and wasn't into horseplay. He'd leave after a game with his parents."

John's freshman college roommate echoed the

description of John as not as closely connected with buddies as other guys. Tad and John were teammates on the high school baseball team and then roommates their first year in college, so they'd spent a lot of time together and shared a lot of experiences. Tad said that John was a "good friend", then added, "but we weren't really close." He went on, "John was a good roommate for me. He helped keep me on the straight and narrow." Tad gave as one of the reasons John didn't tightly bond with teammates and other guys in the dorm is that, "John would never go out to share a brew with friends. John wanted nothing to do with that." After freshman year, Tad said, "We lost track of each other."

-- Heart of a hero --

I did see John Ritter regularly off the basketball court late in the summer before his senior year in high school. And it was strange; the first clue that John's life was not going perfectly well.

Just down the street from me lived a girl. (I'm changing her name.) Jenny was a tomboy. She played in our neighborhood sandlot baseball and football games. She ran around the neighborhood with her collie-dog like a young Amazon in cut-offs and t-shirt. But after her graduation from Parkside Elementary School, she left us younger kids behind to become a dark-haired teenage beauty.

John probably didn't get to know Jenny until they were in high school. Jenny attended Goshen Junior High. John attended Elkhart Township Junior High.

Classmates of John's have told me that John didn't have a girlfriend, or even date, through junior year in high school. A high school friend of John's, who is female, informed me that, "John just didn't seem like dating material, because he was shy around girls and always behaved so properly." But the word around our neighborhood the summer of 1968 was that John and Jenny had started dating. Seems that John fell in love. Jenny didn't. Not with John, anyway.

I don't think John had much experience with personal defeat or with girls by this time in his life. His life revolved around sports and school. His commitment to academic achievement was also "one hundred ten percent". In high school he was routinely on the honor roll and a member of National Honor Society. A fellow member of the Advanced Math and English classes described John as an anomaly, "because most of us were neurotic geeks." He informed me that John had the highest score of anyone in their class on the SAT. In college John would make the Dean's List each semester and graduate with a 3.5 GPA (before grade inflation), was a three-time All-Academic Big Ten Team member, and became an Academic All-American his senior year.

So, John didn't have much time for romance. His days were consumed by sports and school, and like Chip, he worked part-time jobs through high school.

But when he fell, seems he fell hard for Jenny. John pursued her diligently. She blew him off.

The summer before their senior year and into the school year, I often saw John drive down our street past Jenny's house. He was unmistakable, because he drove a late-model convertible with the top down, weather permitting. (I recall rumors that a local car dealership had given or loaned the car to John; and it seemed unlikely his family could afford to buy an expensive late-model car for him. But I refused to believe John Ritter would ever participate in anything that didn't pass the sniff test of the highest moral standards.)

The first couple times he drove by, I waved. John sat rigidly straight with eyes directed ahead. Maybe he didn't see me. He drove by Jenny's house (and mine) day after day, never stopping. It was weird.

I couldn't understand Jenny's choice -- to reject John Ritter! It should have been every girl's dream in town to have John Ritter courting her. Instead, Jenny began dating, went steady with, and married an older guy; a big guy who'd played on the football team.

So, I guess John Ritter, although admired by all the guys, really wasn't "dating material" in high school. The same "girl friend" of John's from high school who said John wasn't dating material explained to me that guys, especially younger ones like me, had a different perspective of John than the girls. "You guys were all so star-struck by him, but young girls are drawn to bad boys. John was the antithesis of that!" She said that John was even "awkward and shy in a crowd". Despite his six foot five inch height, she said John "didn't seem towering until he emerged as the elite athlete on that basketball court." Within the society of the GHS Class of 69, she thought John was so unassuming and behaved so respectfully toward everyone that, "I don't believe John saw himself as mainstream."

The shy-around-girls and unassuming John Ritter must have left Goshen for Indiana University with a broken heart. The elite-athlete John Ritter was expected to help turn around a Hoosiers basketball program, which had descended into mediocrity after retirement of the legendary Branch McCracken. The pressure would be on the three Indiana All-Stars arriving on campus Fall of 1969 to restore IU Basketball to championship form and its winning tradition. At least one would have to handle it without the comfort of a hometown sweetheart.

-- The times, they were a changin' --

By the time John was playing for the Hoosiers, he and Chip Hilton had been demoted in my adolescent mind to relics of embarrassing childhood idolatry. The culturally shattering events of the late 60s had finally reached and riven my hometown. Long hair, rock music, and all the associations and accoutrements of the counter-cultural youth movement had arrived in Goshen. High school kids were smoking pot, dropping acid, and participating in protests on the Goshen

College campus against the war in Viet Nam. We didn't have any black kids in Goshen High School, but we were in solidarity with the civil rights movement too, brother! We started a student-exchange program with Shortridge High School in the Indianapolis inner-city. (It was deeply disappointing that our family got a white kid in the exchange to stay at our house.)

Social-political schisms surfaced that rocked our previously placid community. Peacenik hippies were called sissies ("I bet they squat to piss!") by Korean and World War II vets and Nixon supporters. Viet Nam vets came back from that war with opium-laced pot and joined protests against Nixon's government instead of the American Legion or VFW. Guys with hot cars were no longer so cool. VW bugs with peace-sign stickers and hippie vans competed for spaces with souped-up Chevys and Fords in the high school parking lot.

It was a time of transition. Jocks smoked pot at beer parties. Over one hundred students walked out of classes and rallied in front of the school to protest the high school dress code my junior year. Boys wanted the right to grow mustaches and beards. Girls wanted to be able to wear pants and mini-skirts.

The connection might not have been obvious to our parents, but the inclination to adolescent rebellion in our all-white Midwestern town seemed, to the more imaginative kids in Goshen, somehow relevant to the counter-culture and anti-establishment movements tearing the nation apart.

My own dreams of being like Chip had died a slow, but not an agonizing, death. I still swam and ran track, but more for the comradeship of the team than any expectation of stardom or recognition. The stands were rarely filled with cheering fans at swimming and track meets -- no cheerleaders or booster club -- usually just parents and girlfriends. By senior year my brother and I had sold our tricked-out Plymouth Sport Fury for a beat up old Jag. Like many of my friends in Goshen, by 1970 I had traded in Mickey Mantle for

Mick Jagger.

    I had willfully defected to the other side. Sports and cars, obeying and respecting authority, loyalty to school, community and country -- the civic and cultural values I'd grown up with as a middle-class white kid in small-town Indiana -- were disrupted in the late 1960s. They were, at least temporarily, displaced with those of Peacenik Hippies by 1970. I wanted to be with what was happening Now! I didn't want to be stuck back in the 1950s with Chip Hilton and his gang of school-spirited buddies.

    I dropped out of college after a semester, worked proletarian jobs in factories and construction crews and hitchhiked around the country. When I went back to college I wasn't sure if I was an anarchist or a Marxist, but I knew I wasn't the boy who'd idolized Chip Hilton and been thrilled by John Ritter's congratulations.

    After my own high school graduation I was vaguely aware of John Ritter's accomplishments for the IU Hoosiers, but wasn't especially interested. Except one time. I was visiting friends at IU, who lived in an off-campus apartment in Bloomington. It was John's senior year. I think the Hoosiers were playing University of Kentucky, their arch rivals, in the quarterfinals of the NCAA tournament. And there was John Ritter on the TV set in my friends' squalid student apartment.

    And there we were, screaming and yelling for Ritter, our hometown hero, just like we'd done so many times in the Goshen High School Gym. He still seemed to float majestically above the other, lesser players on the court. He was untouchable, dribbling the ball like a point guard, hitting long-range jump shots, boxing out and grabbing rebounds like a power forward. He could still play any position. It was magical. My long-haired, cynically sophisticated buddies, and me; we were transported back to the Boys Booster Club -- pounding the bleachers and cheering once again for Goshen's greatest. Our real-live Chip Hilton.

Part Two
Disappointment

Chapter Four
Failure to Perform

Watching that basketball game on TV in 1973 is the last memory I have of seeing John Ritter in real time. I have searched the Internet to see what information there is available in the public domain about him during and after his last game at IU. There are surprisingly few references to John Ritter, if you Google him. The hometown hero who seemed larger than life in our small town has not made a ripple large enough in the pond of the greater world to merit a **Wikipedia** bio.

One of the best sources for a summary of John Ritter's basketball achievements while he was in college is the previously referenced Stu Swartz article of Friday, April 4, 2008, in the **Goshen News**. The article is a celebration of the 35th anniversary of Indiana University's NCAA matchup against UCLA, John's penultimate college game. To quote a bit more from it:

An amazing accomplishment during Ritter's junior year at IU was outscoring the entire Notre Dame team ... He tallied 32 points as the Hoosiers romped 94-29 ... Ritter for awhile was the top-free throw shooter in IU history, making 257 of 298 attempts for 86.2 per cent. Steve Alford topped that with 535-of-596 for 89.8 per cent from 1984-87. Ritter was named an Academic All-American in 1973 and was Academic All-Big 10 three times.

Despite these accomplishments, John received, what seems to me, rather nuanced praise from Coach Bob Knight summing up John's contribution to the Hoosiers. From the

Swartz article:

"John Ritter has meant an awful lot to Indiana basketball,' said Knight. *"His play in various games has been outstanding. From start to finish, he has meant as much in leadership as a senior possibly could."*

The best player ever to come out of Goshen, Indiana, only played outstanding in **various games**!?

Of course Bob Knight, the master strategist and judge of basketball talent, could see and evaluate a player in ways mere mortal eyes cannot (especially eyes biased by hometown favoritism). Freshmen at IU John's senior year were seniors three years later when Knight's Hoosiers had the best all-around team in college basketball history. The team was undefeated and won the national championship in 1976.

In retrospect I suppose it's notable that John was named an Academic All-American, not a Basketball All-American. Still, it's hard to accept that Goshen's greatest player couldn't make it in the NBA. That's right; John Ritter did not fulfill the dreams his hometown fans had for him. He failed to live up to our expectations to become a star performer we could watch on television playing in the NBA. Why did he disappoint us?

When I Google search for information about Ritter's NBA career, all I can find of any value is "Apr 24, 1973 - The Cleveland Cavaliers selected John Ritter in Round 8 with Pick 5 in the 1973 NBA Draft. ... Draft Rights Renounced: Sep 1, 1976 Cleveland Cavaliers." (***Real GM***, "John Ritter basketball player") Apparently, John was not seen by the NBA scouts as a top pro prospect. He wasn't drafted until the 8th round. The Cleveland Cavaliers relinquished their rights to him three years later. But John never played an NBA game from what I can gather from Internet searches. The page listing in ***Real GM*** for John's statistics as a pro are completely blank.

Basketball aficionados are aware that there was another pro league which was in competition with the NBA from 1967 until 1976. The American Basketball Association merged with the National Basketball Association after nine years of independence. ***Wikipedia's*** entry for "1973-74 Indiana Pacers season" lists John Ritter in the draft class for the Pacers. The entry is not completely clear, but it appears John was either the eighth pick or picked in the eighth round by the Pacers for the 1973-74 season. But he doesn't show up on the team roster, so he evidently did not sign with the Pacers.

In contrast to what I found through Internet searches, my memory of the talk around Goshen was that Ritter did sign with the Pacers, but got cut before the season started.

Whatever actually happened or didn't happen with John after graduating from IU, I can find no record that he ever played professional basketball in any league.

This was a shocking lesson in relative perspective for Ritter fans in Goshen. Our best ever wasn't good enough to play in the NBA or ABA.

John Ritter's and Larry Bird's similarities in style of play and backgrounds have been noted. Both had incredible touch with the basketball and could swish shot after shot from any spot on the court. They each had such extraordinarily keen vision and "court sense", they could be counted on to hit the open man with a bullet pass. They both had extremely high basketball IQs. A former teammate of John's told me that Ritter and Bird carefully studied the weaknesses of opponents for upcoming games. They out-played more physically gifted athletes, because they knew the other guy's tendencies and weaknesses. They could usually anticipate what their opposite number would do.

But there were significant differences. Bird was four inches taller and bulkier than John. John had to outsmart bigger and stronger opponents. Whereas Bird could play inside and over-power players even in the NBA. John had been able to do that in high school, but at the college level his slender figure required him to play more of a finesse game.

There were also significant socio-economic differences. Larry's hometown of West Baden was a crappy little farm and coal town of a couple hundred souls. (It's now much improved with the restoration of a grand tourist attraction, the West Baden Springs Hotel.) Goshen was the county seat with a diverse and growing economy. Goshen College, a small liberal arts Mennonite college, is located on the edge of town and added a modicum of culture. Larry's family was down right poor, while John's was middle class. Both boys had very close relations with their fathers, but Larry's dad was an alcoholic and couldn't find steady work. John's parents went to all his games, even his little league baseball games. Larry's parents divorced, and then his father shot himself in the head so the family would receive his life insurance when Bird was eighteen.

    Larry Bird was left bewildered, hurt, and angry by his father's suicide. Bird dropped out of IU to work as a garbage collector. When he left behind a career in trash removal to emerge from his self-imposed exile from school and basketball, he played angry. Bird sublimated his pain and took it out on opponents on the basketball court by beating them with creative play or sheer grit and determination or physical domination; whatever it took to win.

    John was very intense, when he played ball, but he didn't play angry. His temperament was too mild. A former teammate of John's described John's style of play as "too careful for the NBA". Instead of a father who left him hurt and angry, John's father came to every practice and game. Instead of anger sublimated into a rage to win, John felt pressured to perform perfectly.

    Maybe, as John indicated in that interview after his final college game, the pressure had become too great a burden to bear. The pressure to perform perfectly, to win, to succeed, to achieve, to represent Goshen, the IU Hoosiers, the State of Indiana, Bob Knight, to please his father -- perhaps the only way for John to release the pressure was to get out of basketball.

    But Chip always found a way to deal with the

pressures he was under. Why couldn't our real live hometown hero?

-- Our State's religion --

In small towns in Indiana, Basketball is the State Religion. The teenagers that play on the high school team may feel the pressure of representing their school and town even more deeply than the high school principal or town mayor. The performance of these teenage boys (and since Title IX, girls) is on public display in front of the whole town every week of the cold winter months. In small Midwestern towns there isn't much to do in the winter if you're not into high school basketball. The gyms are usually full on game night. A town's identity and self-respect is to a large extent placed on the shoulders of these not-yet-fully-formed adolescents.

Driving state highways throughout Indiana when you reach a city boundary you're likely to see a welcome sign proclaiming a long-ago state championship or that it's the hometown of some forgotten outstanding high school athlete. (The movie *Hoosiers* and Hickory High should come to mind. The film was written by Angelo Pizzo and directed by David Anspaugh, two Hoosier boys.) My favorite is the sign welcoming motorists to Swayzee on State Road 13. It boasts that Swayzee is the "state record-holder for the most overtimes in a basketball game" (9 during a March 15, 1964 game). Might not be much, but in Indiana it's something.

Goshen doesn't have a sign memorializing John Ritter's accomplishments. He left us hanging.

Chapter Five

Out of Step with the Culture

    Something terribly unexpected did happen to John Ritter while he was in college at Indiana University. Crucial details were kept from the general public, and I don't think many people in Goshen were aware of it then or now.

    Rebellion against authority was breaking out on campuses all across the US for many different causes. College sports teams were not exempt. There was a revolt of players against the head basketball coach of the IU Hoosiers near the end of the season in 1971, John's sophomore year. John picked, what turned out to be, the wrong side by standing with the coach and opposing the rebels.

    But how could it be otherwise? Chip Hilton would never participate in a revolt against Rock, Chip's coach, or against any legitimate authority. Like John Ritter, Chip would have supported his coach, but he would have talked his teammates into coming around, and everything would have worked out. That's exactly what John Ritter tried to do. Because that's what a good guy from Goshen, Indiana, with solid Midwestern values and "the right stuff" was supposed to do.

    Unlike Chip's fictional world of the 1950s, it didn't work out that way for John in 1971. His teammates thought John was standing on the wrong side of a line they drew.

-- *Loyalty* --

    John was not recruited to play for the IU Hoosiers by Bobby Knight. Knight was hired as head coach of the Indiana University Basketball Team at the start of the 1971-72 season, John's junior year. John was actually recruited and initially coached by Knight's predecessor, Lou Watson.

Coach Watson was the keynote speaker at the Goshen High School letterman's banquet John's senior year in high school. I was in attendance as a sophomore "G-Man" as I won my letter on the swimming team in 1969. My memory of Watson's speech is very vague (as mentioned above, until corrected, my memory was that Coach Wooden was the speaker). I do recall that much of the talk was directed at and about John Ritter. Watson must have been overjoyed that John was coming to Bloomington instead of going to LA.

In basketball-crazy Indiana, "Lou Watson" is the answer to a Trivial Pursuit question: Who was the IU coach in between Branch McCracken, who coached two national championship teams, and Bob Knight, who coached three national championship teams?

Under McCracken and later Knight, the Hoosiers were a dominant team in the Big Ten Conference and regular contenders for a national title. Watson was the IU head coach for five years from 1965-66 to 1970-71. He had a winning record -- barely -- losing sixty games and winning sixty-two. During Watson's tenure as head coach, IU managed to share a conference title in the Big Ten and finished third place in the NCAA regional tournament. His was an unexceptional record, but at most universities Coach Watson would have been considered an adequate coach. Not in Indiana, where our sense of self-worth depends on winning basketball games.

Lou Watson should have been perfect for Indiana University. He was a Hoosier through and through. He was the star of his Jeffersonville High School team. Joined the Navy immediately after graduation in 1944 and participated in D-Day storming the beaches of Normandy with the Marines. He made it onto the IU Basketball Team as a twenty-two year-old freshman. Under Coach McCracken the six foot five inch forward became the career-leading scorer for IU, was named to the Big Ten's All-Conference Team and a Third Team All-American. Watson's coaching career followed a natural progression. His first job was assisting Branch McCracken. Watson left IU to become a successful small-town coach for Huntington High School (Vice President Dan Quayle's hometown). Lou Watson returned to Indiana University for another stint as McCracken's assistant with the understanding he was being groomed to succeed his mentor.

When Lou Watson became head coach of the Hoosiers in 1965 it must have seemed like a story-book tale come true for IU fans. Who was more of a true-blue Hoosier than this guy! And who better prepared than the great Branch McCracken's long-time and loyal assistant? But the times they were a changin' and not all basketball players in the late 1960s fit the mold of the Chip Hilton-like Lou Watson, or John Ritter.

Lou Watson died March 24, 2012 at the age of eighty-eight. The following day, in a backhanded sort of tribute to Watson, *Inside Indiana Hoosier Sports Nation* posted an article, "Sign of the Times", by Ken Bikoff, which was originally published by *Inside Indiana Magazine* earlier that year. Bikoff's article contains research and interviews, which paint a sympathetic yet tragic picture of Watson. Much of the content had not been made public before the original publication in 2012.

When John Ritter was a freshman at IU in 1969-70, first-year students were not allowed to play varsity basketball by rule of the NCAA. That year, Coach Watson was hospitalized with severe back pain. Surgeries and painful recuperation forced him to turn over the reins of the Hoosiers to assistant coach Jerry Oliver. With Watson's return in 1970 and three Indiana High School All-Stars, Ritter, George McGinnis, and Steve Downing, now eligible as sophomores, the mouths of IU fans were watering in anticipation of a run for a championship in the 1970-71 season.

The team lived up to its hype and the expectations of its alumni boosters -- for awhile. After a string of victories, tough breaks and bad calls by referees began to derail the Hoosiers from their charge toward a Big Ten championship and national tournament bid. The first bad break was against the hated Kentucky Wildcats. From Bikoff's article:

Indiana appeared to pull off a major upset of No. 3 Kentucky Dec. 12 in Bloomington when Ritter drained a 55-foot desperation shot at the buzzer to give Indiana an apparent 82-80 win, but the shot was waved off because McGinnis had called timeout before Ritter's shot. Ritter missed a second chance at a game-winner, and UK went on to win in overtime 95-93.

Nevertheless, the Hoosiers rolled on through the season with an outstanding record of seventeen wins and only four losses, and a Big Ten Conference record of 8-2. The stage was set for a deciding conference title-game with Ohio State on March 9. IU would need to beat Wisconsin and Iowa before the crucial battle with the Buckeyes, but those teams were not expected to be stumbling blocks in the Hoosiers run for the championship.

But instead of winning a statement game in Madison, the Hoosiers imploded. They led 71-66 with 5:07 to play, but they failed to score the rest of the way in regulation. Along the way IU missed a lay-up, three free throws and two more shots in the paint, and McGinnis missed an open 22-foot jumper. At the end of regulation with the score tied at 71, Indiana had a chance to win when Wisconsin's Glen Richgels missed a 20-footer in the final seconds. IU's Wright and Rick Ford went up for the rebound, and Richgels was called for a foul at the buzzer. It should have sent Ford to the free-throw line for two potential game-winning shots, but officials ruled the foul came after the buzzer. In fact, they waved off Richgels' shot as well. Indiana went on to lose 94-87 in double overtime. (Bikoff, "Sign of the Times," **Inside Indiana Hoosier Sports Nation**, March 25, 2012)

Indiana did go on to trounce Iowa. But instead of a campus-wide celebration, students paraded around the IU Fieldhouse with signs demanding Coach Watson's ouster. In response, Watson called a meeting of the players and told them he would resign, if that was what the team wanted. In their coach's presence the players voiced their support for him. But just a day later several of the African-American players met in secret and decided they did want a change. They requested the help of an Urban Studies professor, John Brown. Ten of the fourteen varsity players (including some white players and excluding McGinnis) asked Brown to represent them and speak to Watson about complaints they had. Interestingly, racial bias was not among the stated complaints.

The chapter on the 1970-71 season in the *Indiana University Basketball Encyclopedia, 2nd Ed.*, Jason Hiner, December 13, 2013, Skyhorse Publishing, Inc., relates that the complaints of the players against Coach Watson that were relayed to the coaching staff through Professor Brown included, "not teaching them enough about basketball, having a lack of team discipline, and showing favoritism toward John Ritter and George McGinnis." The initial meetings of the players with Brown and between Brown and Watson were kept confidential among the participants and not leaked to the press. Later George McGinnis did join the rebels and participated in subsequent meetings in solidarity with his teammates. A few of the players argued that they should boycott the game against Ohio State. They were out-voted.

What was John Ritter's role in the uprising? When student-fans demonstrated their discontent with Coach Watson, Chip Hilton would have found a way to calm the waters and rally the team around the coach. That's exactly what Ritter tried to do. He drafted a letter from the players to the local newspaper supporting the coach. Not a single player agreed to sign it. John was so far out of touch with his teammates that he was excluded from the team meetings to discuss grievances. According to the Bikoff article, John Brown informed Ritter that, since John's views were so different than his teammates, he was not welcome at the meetings.

Lou Watson's story-book rise to head coach of his

beloved IU Hoosiers ended the night before the game against Ohio State. He tendered his resignation. IU was soundly thumped by the Buckeyes 91-75. John Ritter did not score a single point.

From Bikoff's "Sign of the Times":

*Ritter, meanwhile, was livid about what had happened, and he initially vowed to sit out the Illinois game in protest. (There was one game left in the season after the Ohio State game, IU vs. Illinois.) "I wanted him to stay," Ritter told the H-T (local newspaper, **Bloomington Herald-Telephone**, which reported on Watson's resignation). "He's one of the big reasons I came to Indiana. After the way the guys felt, and the way they acted, I just feel they have a better chance of winning without me. I was against this 150 percent. So I'm not going to be playing Saturday. I'll decide about my future here later." Ritter also added that he tried to attend a team meeting early in the day Wednesday, but he was asked to leave by Professor Brown after he said that he didn't agree with what the rest of the team was doing. Eventually Ritter was talked out of his protest by Orwig (IU Athletic Director), and he would suit up for IU vs. Illinois. (parentheticals added)*

Indiana was thrashed by Illinois 103-87 to end the disastrous 1970-71 season. Enter Army's coach, Bob Knight, the following season to crack the whip and restore discipline to the IU program for John Ritter's final two years as a basketball player.

Chapter Six

Estrangement from Community

Eight of the fifteen players on the IU basketball team for the 1970-71 season were African-American. All the participants on both sides of the player revolt publicly denied that race was a factor in the dispute between the players and Coach Watson. The president of Indiana University, John Ryan, told the local press that there were "no racial issues" involved in Watson's resignation. Bikoff's article, however, suggests that racial tension might have been a factor. After all, it was 1971.

Considering the racial problems suffered by the football team just two years earlier when 10 black players were dismissed from the team after boycotting some practices, Ryan's denial of any racial issues can be expected. ... After all, players both black and white had turned against Watson in a united front.

That said, Ruf (reporter on the story in 1971 for the **Indiana Daily Student***) says that after looking over the reporting he did more than 40 years ago, a racial element manages to leak through. "I didn't think at the time that there was anything racially involved, but as I was reading those clips, all of a sudden it seemed curious to me that all the white players came out first," Ruf says. (referring to a meeting held at IU President John Ryan's house with the players at which Ryan informed the team that Watson had resigned) "Then there was another group of white guys who came out about 10 minutes later. About 15 minutes after that, all the black guys came out with the faculty advisor (Professor Brown). At the time, it never occurred to me that there was anything racially involved, but maybe there was." (parentheticals added)*

Whether race was a factor or not, the social-cultural upheaval of the late 1960s and early 70s was. It is almost inconceivable that players would have revolted against their coach in the 1950s and early 60s the way the IU players did in 1971. They used the tactics employed by the civil rights and antiwar movements. A popular, at least with black students, urban studies professor was brought in as their advocate. Demands were made. A boycott was considered. Those not sufficiently radical and committed to the cause were ignored and excluded. Just because they were college athletes didn't mean they hadn't learned from the civil rights and peace movements.

America was divided back then. The divisions were generational and racial. It was the anti-authoritarian youth and pissed-off blacks against the adult establishment. The angry Silent Majority was furious that the coddled kids of the Baby Boom generation didn't just shut up and do what their parents, teachers, coaches, and other authority figures told them to do. And, it was baffling to these folks why blacks were not grateful for the progress that had been made in civil rights. Didn't black people have (in theory) equal rights under the law?!

Bikoff's article captures the attitude of supporters of the Establishment toward rebellious youth and minorities by quoting from a columnist's response in the **Indianapolis Star** to the player revolt.

... the players took plenty of criticism from the media about the way they acted. Max Stultz, a columnist for the Indianapolis Star, laid into the players about their actions. "The coach has to decide -- right or wrong -- who plays and how much," Stultz wrote in the March 12 edition of the Star. "That's his responsibility. He must answer to his boss, not to a bunch of guys in short pants whose loyalty doesn't extend past their reflection in a mirror. ... I have little respect for trouble-makers who, instead of realizing their own shortcomings and try to improve, grab a crying towel and head for the nearest sympathetic ear."

The grumpy-patronizing-dismissive tone of the Stultz column was typical of the outrage expressed by Nixon's "silent majority" about the insurrections against established authority sweeping across the country in inner-city neighborhoods and college campuses. Bus boycotts, freedom rides, and anti-war rallies were linked to Communist conspiracies and treason in the minds of many of the World War II generation. J. Edgar Hoover was not alone in believing Martin Luther King, Jr., was a dangerous pinko.

The generation gap wasn't just about hair length and right/left politics. It was about the soul of the country. Was control to be left to those in power, The Establishment? Or were The People to have a voice? Were minorities to be given a place at the table in deciding government policies and law? Should the concerns of students be considered in developing academic curricula and campus social-regulations?

The right to vote is taken for granted by Millennials. But throughout the 1960s 18-year olds were being drafted and sent to fight in Viet Nam without the right to vote until they were twenty-one. The 26th Amendment finally reduced the legal voting age from 21 to 16 in 1971. Hell yes, young people were pissed off at the "grown ups" during the 60s.

Voices of the previously powerless were speaking out loudly, and sometimes violently, from Watts to Harvard Yard. Twenty year-olds at Indiana University, scholarship athletes they might be, were not unaffected by the zeit geist of those times.

John Ritter and Chip Hilton were not of those times. John was a living, breathing human being existing in the space-time continuum of the late 1960s and early 70s. But who he was when he joined the IU Hoosiers Basketball Team had been shaped and molded by the relatively unchanged life of small-town Indiana, not in a smoldering inner-city or on a restless campus. John lived on the cusp of change, but, until that season of turmoil in 1970-71, John seems to have been unaffected by the swirling cultural tumult around him.

All hell broke loose in Goshen High School the year after John's graduation. The wave of revolution against authority even reached our placid shores. Over a hundred high school kids walked out of school to protest the dress code. Some of the most popular girls in the school did not try out for cheerleading and did not apply to join Sunshine Society and Rainbow (the social clubs which the proper young ladies of Goshen all joined by tradition). A few of the boys who were good athletes didn't go out for the high school teams and several quit Boy Scouts and DeMolay. Good god! What was happening to the social order in our town?

Well, some of the kids a year or more behind John in school decided that there were alternatives to the traditional extra-curricular activities of school clubs, sports, cheerleading, choir, band, orchestra, and working on cars. Hippie guys and chicks were into growing their hair, smoking pot, taking drugs, listening to psychedelic rock, and driving their VW vans to outdoor rock concerts. Political activists were organizing and attending peace rallies, protest marches, and walks for hunger. Jesus freaks were organizing and attending prayer circles and love-ins. But John Ritter had left town to live in the jocks' dorm and play on the freshman team at IU.

Still, as a freshman at IU in 1969 he would have encountered far more radical behavior than high school kids protesting the school dress code. John would have been exposed to radical feminists fighting for women's liberation. The gay rights movement was already active at IU in 1969, the year of the Stonewall Riots. Sexual liberation was in the air and in practice now that students had access to The Pill. Political activity was charged with anger and fear. The Viet Nam War was grinding on without an end in sight. The Student Deferment from Selective Service ended in 1970, so college students would be subject to the Draft Lottery. No more dodging the Draft by staying in school.

Radical Leftists, hippies, Yippies, and dropouts that hung out around university campuses were all part of the college scene in the late 60s and early 70s. IU was no exception. Radical politics were as extreme at Indiana as any major state university. William and Emily Harris met at IU and became founding members of the notorious Symbionese Liberation Army. The SLA later made international news for the kidnapping of Patty Hearst, murder, and armed bank-robbery. Their crime spree was part of a twisted vision of how to bring about a Maoist-Marxist revolution in the US.

Not all IU students were into radical politics or hippie counter-culture. Traditional college life was still available at IU, and many kids experienced college much like previous generations. Students pledged Greek societies, partied, and studied for exams. They cheered for the home team at ball games and looked up to jocks. But this way of life was no longer the dominant vision of how to spend four years within the ivy-covered walls of what was supposed to become one's beloved alma mater. Greek life and school spirit made a come back in the 1990s, but most of the Baby Boom generation, John Ritter's generation, rejected many of the traditions associated with life on a college campus. Many Boomers preferred to let their hair down, smoke weed, listen to Jimi Hendrix, and make love not war, rather than join the Booster Club.

-- Alienation of a traditional conformist out of respect for authority --

Along with not being into the cultural revolution of the 60s, another aspect of John Ritter's alienation from the discontent of his teammates might have been a certain type of self-righteous conformism. John was a good guy, a "straight arrow"; too straight to fit in with teammates, led by an African-American professor, challenging authority. John was "good" by the old standards, the same way Chip Hilton had been a good guy in the 1950s. Love of country, loyalty, humility, the virtues held to in the fictional town of Lake Wobegon described by Garrison Keillor in *Prairie Home Companion* -- or maybe by the folks Barack Obama, when he was a presidential candidate in 2008, rather unfortunately said "cling to guns and religion" -- John Ritter was "good" in that cultural milieu. That style of traditional 1950s small-town American virtuousness, which Chip Hilton exemplified, was completely out of step with the counter-cultural revolution roiling state university campuses, like IU, when John Ritter matriculated in 1969.

At the end of John's senior year in high school there were a couple incidents which call into question how tightly bonded he was with teammates on the high school baseball team. My memory of the first incident has faded, is based on hearsay, and I haven't been able to corroborate it. But what I recall being told by a sophomore member of the GHS Baseball Team in the Spring of 1969, when John was a senior and co-captain of the team, is this. There was a beer party involving players on the baseball team. John got wind of it, found out which members of the team went to the party, and informed the coaching staff. A couple players were disciplined or suspended from the team.

Three members of the team I've spoken with have no recollection of John turning in teammates for drinking at a beer party in Goshen. They think my memory of this incident is a false one, or it is an altered version of another incident that happened out of town during the team's spring trip. But one member of the team said that he could well imagine John doing that, "because John was so straight."

The out-of-town incident they do remember is that a bunch of the guys on the baseball team went to a strip club in Louisville during a team trip to Jeffersonville, Indiana. Players on the Jeffersonville team invited their guests from Goshen to join them on an excursion across the Ohio River to see what one of my sources called a "burlesque show". One team member, "Jack", remembers John sitting in the back of the club looking very uncomfortable, and then informing the coaches about the players' indiscretion. Another doesn't remember John being at the strip club.

Jack insists John was there and then confessed to the

coaching staff. Jack quit the team the next year as a consequence of participating in the student "strike" against the high school dress code. He says that he thought of John as a "suck-up" to the coaches. "Ritter seemed more like a member of the coaching staff than a player to me. He related better to adults than the guys on the team." Jack was two years behind John in school and was one of the first jocks at GHS to feel the pull of the cultural revolution creeping toward Goshen. "The coaches brushed it under the table, and nobody got in trouble. They couldn't afford to punish the whole team," Jack concluded.

    I've spoken with the coach of the team, Ken Mirer, about the incident and he has no recollection of it whatsoever. He affirmed the Goshen boys were staying in the homes of Jeffersonville players, and "he didn't know everything they might have gotten up to." He understood that John could have been perceived as closer to him than other guys on the team, especially by a younger member of the team. "John injured his wrist early in the season, so I used him as our first base coach. He was such a smart ball player and the kind of kid that wanted to help the team every way he could."

    If it's true that John ratted on guys for breaking team rules (and the law) against drinking or entering a strip club, he was probably more orthodox in his commitment to following rules than Chip Hilton would have been. It would have been a classic ethical dilemma for Chip -- one of the challenges created for him to overcome in a Clair Bee plot. Is the deeper loyalty owed to your teammates or to your duty as captain to enforce the rules?

    Chipper would have found a way not to squeal on his teammates, but to show them the error of their ways and bring them back onto the path of righteousness. Perhaps John tried, but none of the versions of rule violations I heard included any attempt on John's part to protect his teammates from the consequences of their rule-breaking. From a strict view of John's duty as captain of the team, why should he?

The offending players knew the rules, knew that they were breaking rules, and knew what the consequences could be if they got caught.

If John attended the burlesque show, and confessed his own participation, he can't be accused of being a hypocrite. Perhaps what John was trying to do in the strip club incident was exactly what Chip would've done. Go along with the team on their illicit jaunt, if that's what the guys were determined to do, and then turn yourself in. Chip probably would have volunteered to be the first to take the worst punishment the coaches would dish out. Maybe that's how John expected it to play out.

What I'm sure John's teammates didn't expect was that a teammate would turn them in. Anyone who's watched the TV show *Friday Night Lights*, or seen the movie, will have a pretty good picture of how rules are bent in small towns to protect high school athletes. Seems that within John Ritter's value system, rules should not be bent to accommodate high school booze parties or attending burlesque shows. Most of us might agree with that in the abstract, but that's not how it normally works in communities. Whether it's your family, the Fraternal Order of Police, La Cosa Nostra, or just a small town, we tend to want to protect our own from harsh consequences. Few parents turn in their own kids for breaking the law. If you're a member of a tight community, it's expected that the community will look out for its members and take care of their own. Being on a team means your teammates have your back and you have theirs.

The second incident involved John leaving the baseball team in a time of need. I first learned about this from a good buddy of mine who was a sophomore member of the team. He told me that John faced a dilemma.

Goshen won the sectional baseball tournament the first time in school history John's sophomore year. The team repeated his junior and senior years. Our baseball team had never won the regional tournament until John's senior, and then, they did it! What a thrilling year for the basketball and baseball teams in 1969! With John as co-captain and senior leader on both teams, Goshen won regional tournaments. Two firsts in GHS sports history.

What happened next turned the experience from thrilling into, what Coach Mirer termed "bitter sweet". John Ritter was called up to participate in practices with the Indiana Basketball All-Stars to prepare for the annual game against the Kentucky High School All-Stars. The dilemma John faced was whether to play with the All-Stars or play in the Semi-State baseball tournament. John chose the Indiana All-Stars. His high school baseball team lost in the first round of the semi-state tournament without him.

Should John have remained with the baseball team to help try to win a state championship, which Goshen had never won in any sport, or join the Indiana Basketball All-Stars to practice for the upcoming matchup against the Kentucky All-Stars? John was a graduating senior. His future was in basketball at Indiana University, not in baseball. Practicing with the All-Stars would be John's first chance to get to know and play with George McGinnis and Steve Downing, his soon to be teammates at IU. The pride of Indiana is on the line every year, when our best high school basketball players take on the boys from our State's nemesis across the Ohio River.

Baseball finishes a distant third behind basketball and football in Hoosier sports priorities. So, John's choice might seem obvious and not so difficult to make. Do whatever it takes to help Indiana beat Kentucky.

But that's not how Coach Mirer of the GHS Baseball Team and some of John's teammates saw it. Mel (false name) said, "The only criticism I ever heard Coach Mirer make of John Ritter was when he left the team for the All-Stars practices. He knew it really hurt our chances in the tournament." Mel went on to explain that he didn't think John took the decision lightly, and he "can't blame John for the decision he made." Another member of the team confided that John's pitching was sorely missed, but he doesn't remember any criticism of John by Coach Mirer or teammates for the way he resolved his predicament.

I found an article in the ***Indianapolis Star*** which presents John's point of view.

Ritter Makes Sacrifice To Join Hoosier Team, By Harrison Howard.

"I feel, like I'm letting down all 18 guys on the baseball team," Goshen's contribution to the Indiana All-Star game, John Ritter, stated. "But there was more pressure on me to play in the All-Star game than in the state baseball tourney. "We have a block of 300 people coming down to the game, you know. I really had a tough time making the decision but Coach Mirer (baseball Coach Ken Mirer) finally helped me make up my mind," Ritter added. "He Told me I'd be letting down all those local people if I didn't go to the All-Star game."

... IHSAA rules forbid a player from practicing for an all-star game and still playing high school sports. Following Tuesday's baseball action Ritter really gave it plenty of thought, talked with some coaches in between a flurry of phone calls urging him to play in the All-Star game then drove to Indianapolis in time for practice yesterday morning. ... Ritter, a top student at Goshen, will attend Indiana University this fall. (***The Indianapolis Star***, June 12, 1969, Page 63)

John's description of Coach Mirer's role conflicts with Mel's recollection as well as the Coach's. I had a long conversation with Ken Mirer in which the coach shared tender reminiscences about John Ritter. The only point in which the voice of John's old coach had the tiniest edge to it was his reaction to my description of the content of the ***Star*** article. His reaction to John's statement that he encouraged John to leave the baseball team: "I guess John had his own interpretation."

Coach Mirer told me that John was under a lot of pressure to join the All-Stars. "Lou Watson came to all our practices that spring just to make sure John was okay and stayed committed to Indiana Basketball." John's mother even put the squeeze on Mirer, asking him to tell John "to go with the All-Stars."

Mirer's own recollection is that he tried not to put any pressure on John, but "wished he had accepted the honor (of being named to the All-Stars) but played in the baseball game." Coach Mirer explained that John was uniquely valuable to the team because of his leadership and because he could pitch and play first base or short stop. "John didn't have the greatest fastball, but he threw with pinpoint accuracy. He wasn't the best hitter on the team, but he found ways to get on base better than anyone else on the team. He was a difference maker for us."

Ken Mirer's upbeat and enthusiastic coaching personality lit up the phone line during most of our conversation, but his tone changed recalling how his baseball team's season ended over forty-five years ago. The team was on a roll and full of confidence going into the Semi-State, "But when we lost John it was a real let-down for the team." He called the IHSAA's rule "stupid and unfair." Mirer thinks it was unfair to John to put him in that position and under that pressure. He also thinks the rule was unfair to the baseball team and the other guys on the team.

The most significant factor in John's decision, according to John's explanation in the *Star* article, was pressure. "[T]here was more pressure on me to play in the All-Star game than in the state baseball tourney." If in John's mind even Coach Mirer was encouraging him to "go to the All-Star game," then all the pressure of the adult world was pushing John in that direction. He did make a Chipper-like admission in stating, "I feel like I'm letting down all 18 guys on the baseball team." But the people he consulted appear to be the adults, not buddies on the team. He "talked with some coaches in between a flurry of phone calls urging him to play in the All-Star game."

The guys John was supposedly bonded with were his fellow baseball players. He didn't even personally know the other high school All-Stars. They'd never played together before. The greater loyalty John must have felt was to the higher authority of the sports establishment of Indiana, not to his high school teammates. His priority of values was in sync with that of the higher authorities.

We might think, if it was another kid, the reason was simply selfishness -- he loved basketball more than baseball and making the All-Stars was a bigger deal than high school baseball. That was probably a factor with John. But John Ritter is described by teammates and coaches (including Mirer) as one of those rare athletes who was an utterly unselfish team player. Chip Hilton would not have resolved the ethical dilemma based on selfish motives, and I doubt that John Ritter did.

Now, I think most any Hoosier boy in John's position would have made the same choice he did. But it is notable that the bond with the guys he'd sweated and strived with for four years to bring the baseball team to the point of having Goshen's first chance to win a state championship was not as strong as John's sense of duty and obligation to the Indiana sports establishment. It was the established authorities which most influenced his decision.

John's conformity to duty and loyalty to higher authority is what estranged John from the rest of the team at IU when revolution was brewing. How could he resolve the ethical dilemma of competing loyalties -- to his teammates or to his coach? From the outside, it looks like John valued duty to authority over the comradeship of teammates on the high school baseball team. It also appears that he remained a stickler about obedience to authority at IU. I imagine that in John's mind he was being true to his principles and maintaining his personal integrity by siding with authority. I wonder to what extent he cared about and considered the consequences for relations with his teammates.

    When he came to a fork in the road in college, John stuck to the same path he'd been on in high school. John followed the adult-authorities, not his teammate-peers. I suspect John's IU teammates might have agreed with Jack's characterization of John as a suck-up more comfortable with the coaches than with his peers. Not a problem so long as all the kids followed John as their leader. But when his Hoosier teammates deviated from the straight and narrow path John Ritter strode, he found himself walking alone. When the guys realized that John did not have their backs, they ostracized him.

Chapter Seven

A Hero Walks a Lonely Road

John Ritter played ball with an elegance that made other players look clumsy as they huffed and grunted around him. His grace-filled separateness wasn't limited to athletic ability. He walked the hallways of Goshen High School a head taller than the other boys and with an unassuming confidence uncommon for a teenager. John Ritter wasn't threatening or intimidating even though he was bigger and better than us younger and smaller creatures. He always looked just right, perfectly groomed with upright posture. He was never out of line. He behaved exactly the way parents, teachers, and coaches carped at the rest of us to be. John Ritter appeared to be faultless as a model citizen and student.

But by 1971, when the turmoil on the IU team began, John Ritter was no longer the perfect role model for his peers and younger kids. The traditional values of the 1950s, which set the standards John lived by, were out of date and old fashioned. To counter-culture activists, and even to John's own rebellious teammates, the golden boy from Goshen must have seemed like an alien being in 1971.

So, his teammates excluded him from the planning meetings to work up a list of grievances to present to the IU coaching staff. John wasn't allowed to participate in the negotiations between the university administration and the players mediated by Professor Brown. Despite that John Ritter was the kind of guy you could depend on to be honest and sincere about where he stood, and about knowing right from wrong, he was perceived as not a team player off the court by his teammates. He was the one who was out of line, estranged from the fellowship of the team.

John's over-riding commitment to the value of loyalty to authority separated him from the guys who wanted change and were willing to rebel against the established authorities to make it happen.

Recognizing that he was the misfit, not the disloyal-to-authority rule-breakers, John told the local newspaper that he would not play in the final game of the 1970-71 season and he might feel compelled to leave Indiana University. "After the way the guys felt, and the way they acted, I just feel they have a better chance of winning without me. I was against this 150 percent. So I'm not going to be playing Saturday. I'll decide about my future here later." (Ritter quoted in the Bikoff article, original source ***Bloomington Herald-Telephone***)

But he did play in that game and John's loyalty to Indiana, the State and University, coupled with urging by incoming coach Bob Knight, convinced him to remain at IU for his junior and senior years of eligibility. He probably could have transferred to UCLA, given how hard Coach John Wooden tried to recruit Ritter in high school. John would have been a member of national championship teams had he originally signed with the UCLA Bruins or transferred his junior year. Wooden's teams won the NCAA Tournament every year Ritter was in college. (In fact, the Bruins won consecutive national titles from 1967 through 1976 under Coach Wooden.)

Despite being alienated from teammates and that he was a square peg in the round hole of the cultural mix at IU, John Ritter stuck. His loyalty to Indiana must have overcome the misgivings he had about continuing to play with the guys who rebelled against Coach Watson. They ostracized John, he wavered, but in the end, he stuck with the team. But was it with his fellow players as human beings that John stuck, or was it to a commitment of obedience to authority that he stuck? Did John share a bond of brotherhood with the guys, or was his commitment to an abstract principle of duty? Maybe Bob Knight's commanding personality impressed John.

The quotes in the Bikoff article evidence real feelings in John. He was angry and felt betrayed by his teammates. He expressed earnest devotion to his coach. What is not expressed is a close connection with the guys he sweated, played, and showered with. Just the opposite. He was "150 percent" out of sync with his teammates.

John's loyalty might be interpreted as deep feelings for Coach Lou Watson. "I wanted him to stay ... He's one of the big reasons I came to Indiana." (Bikoff article, quoting John from an interview with the *Bloomington Herald-Telephone*) But was it for Watson as a human being who John sincerely cared about, or did John want Watson to remain the coach because that would preserve the status quo? How bound up was John's allegiance to Coach Watson with a vision in John's mind of how things are supposed to be?

What I'm wondering is to what extent had John Ritter divorced himself from the blood and guts of human relations in his commitment to playing the role of a Chip Hilton-like character on and off the court. By 1971 there must have been a sort of unreality about John's "perfection" in the eyes of his contemporaries. Nevertheless, John Ritter remained in character regardless of the changes happening all around him. John remained true to the script playing the Chip Hilton-like role he had been assigned by destiny, or choice. No matter that the scenery and supporting actors had changed,

So, John stayed at IU after Bob Knight took the reins from Lou Watson. John played a principal role his junior and senior years under Knight helping to rebuild Hoosier Basketball. Maybe all was well with him and any problems with his teammates were suppressed under the strict discipline of "the General". But I can't help thinking that the 1971 player rebellion was a crossroads in John's life. He could have changed his position and joined his teammates in their demands, as George McGinnis did. Instead, John remained steadfastly loyal to Coach Watson, even though that meant he stood alone.

Somehow, John reintegrated into the fellowship of the team under Coach Knight and was elected co-captain his senior year. Steve Downing has described John as one of the most driven and "the smartest" player on the team. In the 1980s I played recreation league ball with a couple players Knight coached several years after Ritter and Downing graduated. Both of them told me that players either thrived under Coach Knight's heavy hand or they left. "You weren't going to have it your way. It was Coach's way or the highway," a member of Indiana's 1981 NCAA championship team explained to me.
     Bob Knight certainly had his faults as a coach and human being, but his reputation for running a no-nonsense and clean program at Indiana remains untainted. Given John's rejection of any basketball program with the slightest moral taint, and his desire to play on a team "you had to work your butt off", Knight's coaching style may have been the therapy John and the team needed to cure any lingering ills after Watson's resignation. But, if it was therapeutic, then why was it such a relief for John to be finished playing at IU, as he disclosed in the interview after his last game?
     His conflict with teammates and John's banishment from team meetings in 1971 had to have rocked John's world. He was isolated, and he considered leaving Indiana University. McGinnis, who was the only other player singled out in the complaints of the rebels for receiving preferential treatment by Watson, did leave to go pro with the Pacers. By sticking it out at IU John stayed in character as Chipper's alter ego. But John must have realized that the reality of 1971 no longer worked the way it had for Chip Hilton or how it was supposed to work for John Ritter. The guys should have followed his example. The team should have rallied around the coach, and then everything would be back to normal. Lou Watson should not have felt the need to resign. IU should not have had to replace Watson with Knight.
     The turn of events John experienced during the 1970-71

season were not supposed to occur in John Ritter's Chip Hilton-like story. But John soldiered on. Of course he did; what would Chip do?

The rejection by Jenny in 1968 might have been the first deviation from the scripted storybook life John seemed to be living. The surprising rejection by his teammates in 1971 must have dealt an even more significant blow to John's self-understanding. A wobble was initiated in John Ritter's carefully plotted orbit.

I don't know whether John read the **Chip Hilton Sports Series** books or not. But the pressure of playing at IU that John was glad to be released from -- maybe it wasn't just playing for Bob Knight. Maybe the pressure from which John needed a release was feeling like he always had to play the role of The Good Guy, always doing the right thing.

What a relief it might have been for John just to let go at some point; to go out with the guys and "share a brew". Get a little dirty and commit a few sins; maybe that would have released the pressure he felt building up inside himself.

In high school, almost everyone admired John Ritter. Yet, he didn't seem to have any really close friends. He hasn't stayed in touch with any high school contemporaries, according to the several classmates and teammates of John I've spoken with. Did he keep peers at a distance, so that they would not perceive he actually wasn't perfect? Perhaps John didn't feel entirely comfortable in the role of the perfect kid.

A kind of funny incident related to me by a friend of John's in high school illustrates how John's exceptional "goodness" created a peculiar sort of detachment in John's relations with other kids. John and "Connie" found themselves the last to leave the library as it was closing. They were classmates and Connie thought of John as a friend. John surprised Connie by asking if she would like to go with him to the drive-in movie. Yikes! The drive-in was where fast kids went to make out. But Connie agreed; she was frankly curious to discover John's intentions.

John behaved like the perfect gentleman. They watched the movie, ate popcorn, and had a nice chat. Connie told me that she wasn't sure, at the time, if the experience qualified as a date or not. She knew John had little experience with girls, and was surprised he had asked her to go out with him. He never asked her out again, so she concluded it wasn't really a date.

Now, there's nothing wrong with the experience Connie describes, except it's just not normal. It's too good to be true. Guys asked girls to go to the drive-in, because they wanted to make out! But John Ritter wasn't normal. He was far better than normal. His gentlemanly behavior with Connie would have been admired by the grown-ups (certainly Connie's father), but considered damn strange by most teenagers.

I think John's "perfection" created a barrier that prevented the closeness of deep, warm friendships. Everyone thought John was a great guy, but no one I've spoken with, including Tad, who was John's baseball teammate and freshman roommate, describes their relationship with John as that of a "close friend".

John Ritter in high school and college was not someone you could confide your innermost secrets and darkest thoughts to, and trust that he could relate to what you were going through. If you did, he probably would have said exactly the right things. But could John actually relate to your feelings of failure, brokenness, or deformity?

Maybe he could have; but who's going to try to relate to a guy on an intimate level that you can't share a beer with?

The world in which a Chip Hilton or John Ritter fit so well as the high school and college sports hero had passed away in the cultural carnage of the late 1960s and early 70s. The world had turned and John Ritter found himself alone as the only voice on the IU Hoosiers Basketball Team holding out to maintain the old order.

Nevertheless, John stayed true to character and stuck to the path of Chip Hilton-like virtue through graduation from IU. Further down the road in life he began to wobble off course even more. And then, he really was isolated.

-- Ain't got no posse --

Allen Iverson, the flashy and controversial NBA player, gave the term "posse" current coinage during his fourteen year-long career. His jewelry bedecked entourage frightened and outraged traditionalist basketball fans. Bling and swagger pushed aside the humble-team-player-attitude American culture had come to expect of our star athletes. This new style of professional athlete played rap music with sagging pants. They partied late and loud. They were called thugs by their elders.

Iverson had to pay a civil judgment in 2007 for a beat down his posse gave a couple other guys. He was publicly criticized by the respected scions of the NBA, like Michael Jordan and Charles Barkley, for hanging out with gangstas instead of his 76ers teammates. But Iverson defended his posse as being his "real friends and family". (See for example, *philly.com*, "`We're Not A Posse' Iverson, Stackhouse Say Followers Are Friends And Family, Not Trouble", Phil Jasner, Daily News Sports Writer, Posted January 28, 1997.)

Chip Hilton had a gang. Speed Morris had dark good looks and a jalopy. (Was he African American?) Biggie Cohen (presumably Jewish) was always there to protect Chip's back on and off the field. Red Swartz and Soapy Smith were the goofballs and class clowns and often the butts of the gang's friendly joshing. Petey Jackson was the soda jerk who served up malts to the guys when they hung out at the lunch counter of the local drug store.

The creator of Chip's crew, Clair Bee, was the Long Island University basketball coach during the 1930s and 40s.

The gang he created is apparently racially and ethnically diverse. Although, the race, religion, or ethnicity of the characters is not specifically mentioned or revealed in the books. Chip considered his buddies to be family and friends, just like Allen Iverson did. They even got into some pushing and shoving matches with rivals.

Chip's gang was created by Clair Bee to represent his ideal of community and fellowship for the 1950s. Allen Iverson's controversial posse made headlines in the late 90s and the first decade of the Millennia. John Ritter's era was in between these two very different cultural epochs.

One of the reasons John didn't have a gang or a posse may have been due to his "good guy" persona not fitting in during the cultural shifts of the late Sixties and early Seventies. But I think the deeper reason was that John did not develop the intimate and caring friendships of regular guys. John's irregular goodness set him apart and put a little distance between him and his fellows.

By the time John Ritter entered IU, Woodstock had happened and Neil Armstrong had walked on the Moon. The trial of the Chicago 7 opened during his freshman year. Changes were happening lightening fast. Sacred temples of cultural traditions were under attack (although many had just been erected during the 1950s) and traditional heroes knocked off their pedestals.

I remember being in a group of kids at the South Side Soda Shop in the Fall of 1969 gathered around a Goshen boy who had been to Woodstock. Somehow Jess (faux name) got to be a stage hand and roadie at Woodstock. He came back home with a dove and guitar embroidered on his blue jean vest. Long-haired kids in Goshen held him in awe. Jess was treated like a rock star, a returning hero.

By the time John Ritter graduated from IU to try to make it on an NBA or ABA team, the 60s were in the rear-view mirror. Woodstock and the peace movement had transmogrified into bitterness and anger over the seemingly endless war in Viet Nam and Hells Angels trashing the Stones' Altamont Rock Festival. Urban neighborhoods had gone up in flames. African-Americans accused Nixon of waving a white flag on the "war on poverty" and civil rights initiatives launched by the Kennedy-Johnson administrations. The Watergate Burglars had committed their foul deeds and Nixon would resign a year after John's graduation. Times had changed, even if he didn't.

When John failed to make it with the Cavaliers or the Pacers, I imagine that he must have felt disappointed and lonely. Failure was not supposed to be part of the John Ritter story.

Was there a gang or posse John could turn to for solace or that had his back? I don't think he had the intimate friendships that bind teammates together as brothers. The internal pressure to be perfect John felt created external pressure which pushed friends just far enough away that John didn't have "close friends".

As we'll see, authority figures at IU and in the business community did offer opportunities to John Ritter after he was finished as a basketball player. But there came a time when John's heart wasn't in it anymore. He threw away the opportunities his outstanding achievements and excellence as a person had earned him. And then, even the authorities to whom he had been loyal turned their backs on him.

Chapter Eight

A Hero Fades from Memory

John Ritter remained at IU and on the basketball team through his junior and senior years, despite being ostracized by his teammates during the player rebellion of his sophomore year. He stuck it out even though the coach who recruited him, and John fought to keep, had left under a cloud of discontent. One of the traditional values John Ritter grew up with in small-town Indiana was that you don't quit. Parents, teachers, and coaches in the 1950s gave moral instruction to boys with aphorisms like, "Quitters never prosper", "The strongest steel is forged in the hottest fire", and "When the going gets tough, the tough get going".

How well did it serve John Ritter to stay true to his school? Did he prosper? Did his steel become stronger?

At first, it seemed so. Ritter served as a building block in Bob Knight's master plan of restoring the IU Hoosiers to their former glory as national championship contenders. John's senior year, Knight's second year at IU, the team had a great run in the NCAA Tournament up to the semi-final game against UCLA. Three years later, with the freshman players John had mentored as a senior now seniors themselves, the Hoosiers won the NCAA title. So, what did John get out of sticking around to help resurrect the Hoosiers to their former glory?

When I finally settled in as an undergrad at the University of Chicago after a couple years of wandering, I still had connections and regular communications with folks back home in Goshen and friends at Indiana University. While my interest in Goshen's Chip Hilton might have waned, if asked, I'm sure I would have said I expected, and I think most Ritter fans in Goshen expected, John would be playing pro basketball somewhere. Surely the best player ever to come out of Goshen, Indiana, coveted by the legendary Wooden for UCLA and a star for Bobby Knight at IU, would sign with a professional basketball team to begin the next stage of his life. When his pro career ended, coaching or business opportunities would open up for John.

That was the script John's fans in Goshen and at IU thought had been written for our Chip Hilton. That's how it would have gone, if John Ritter lived in Chip Hilton's world. But reality may be less predictable, less fair, and less forgiving than fiction.

As noted above, records reveal that John was drafted by the Cavaliers and ABA Pacers, but he didn't play for either team. Word around town was that, instead of going overseas to play in one of the foreign leagues or joining a semi-pro team, Ritter was hired for an executive-track position in Indianapolis with Eli Lilly and Company. "Lilly" was and is one of Indiana's biggest and most prestigious employers. An acquaintance of mine, who worked for Lilly while John was there, told me that the higher-ups in the company "looked upon John Ritter as their golden boy."

I also heard it through the Goshen grapevine that John had married a gal who was a beauty and from a "good family" (probably "old money") in Indianapolis. The Goshen grapevine was not always accurate, but always believed in by its participants right up until clear evidence proved it absolutely wrong.

Whatever was actually happening in John's life, there was surprise and disappointment that our favorite son had not made it in the NBA or ABA. But Ritter fans in Goshen were able to find some satisfaction in learning that our hero had still done well for himself. If basketball was no longer to be his field of conquest, then he would surely go far in business. John had been an A-student, Academic All-American, and majored in Finance. And, he was John Ritter.

So, of course, he'd landed an excellent entry position with a Fortune 500 company right after graduation.

John's Goshen fans could rest assured that he was on his way to success in the business world, and he'd made a match with someone the matrons of our town could be proud. Whatever John Ritter attempted, we all knew he would be a great success.

In the meantime, John's younger brother Mike, who was an outstanding player in his own right for the Redskins, had come back to town as an assistant coach of the high school basketball team. So, at least there was still a Ritter the town could dote on, or criticize, depending on whether "the Skins" were winning or losing.

So much for our former hometown hero. Case closed. Town gossips would have to find new subjects and sports fans new heroes.

Life in Goshen moved on. We really didn't know what was happening in John's life, and we didn't really much care anymore. Had he made it onto an NBA team the community would have followed his progress with keen interest. Talk about how well he was playing, his shooting, rebounding and assists statistics would have been bandied about over cups of coffee at the Olympia Candy Kitchen and ice-cold Cokes at the South Side Soda Shop. But there really wasn't anything more to say about John Ritter. His name would remain all over the high school basketball record book and on trophies in the glassed-in case in the main hall outside the GHS Gym. Pictures of John with the 1968-69 team, when the Redskins made their best-ever run at a state championship, graced the trophy case. But John Ritter and his glory days were beginning to fade from the community's collective memory by the time Goshen's next sports phenom appeared in the 1980s.

Rick Mirer (son of John Ritter's baseball coach, Ken Mirer) passed for 3,973 yards and thirty touchdowns and led the Goshen High School Football Redskins to a state championship his senior year in 1988. He broke the Indiana High School passing record and won the Academy of Achievement Award as the top high school football player in the country in 1989, along with the Atlanta Touchdown Club's Bobby Dodd Award as the nation's best high school quarterback.

Mirer chose to accept a scholarship offer to play for the venerable Notre Dame Fighting Irish rather than IU's desultory football program. His decision paid off. He had an outstanding career with the Irish. It was capped off his senior year with a Cotton Bowl victory in which Notre Dame thrashed Texas A&M 28-3. Rick Mirer accounted for more points running and throwing (350) than any other player in Notre Dame history. He was the second over-all pick in the NFL draft by the Seattle Seahawks. Mirer signed a five year, $15 million contract. The Seahawks had great expectations of their rookie QB. Expectations were fulfilled his first year in the league. Mirer set an NFL record for rookie quarterbacks for pass completions and yards gained.

Unfortunately, Mirer did not become a star quarterback in the NFL. He kind of fizzled after that great rookie season. He never performed at that level again. He did have a journeyman career and hung on for twelve years in the NFL, playing on seven different teams. Rick Mirer deserves to be considered the greatest athlete to come out of Goshen, Indiana, in my lifetime. His success at all levels, in terms of wins and statistical accomplishments, exceeds that of John Ritter, our greatest basketball player.

I remember seeing Rick Mirer on a visit to Goshen one summer weekend when my two sons were tykes. It was around 2005 at the end of Mirer's NFL career. He was dining at another table at Maplecrest Country Club. He graciously signed autographs for the little guys. He seemed well satisfied with life. Mirer's beautiful wife was at his side and he was surrounded by family. Rick's failure to achieve NFL stardom did not seem to have dampened the mood at the Mirer table.

An article in *Sports Entertainment Life*, "Where Are They Now? Rick Mirer", May 30, 2012, relates that Mirer is happily married to Stephanie Mirer, has three children and a dog named Lola. "He now coaches football for the Torrey Pines Pop Warner youth football league and also owns and operates a winery in California's Napa Valley, Mirror Wine Company. A percentage of the proceeds from wine sales benefit his Mirer Family Foundation, which assists children in need in his hometown of Goshen, Ind., and various groups around his current home in San Diego."

Rick Mirer might not have fulfilled his fans highest expectations for success in the NFL, but it seems like his life has gone just about exactly the way it should. By that, I mean it appears from the outside that Rick is getting out of life all the things the good folks of Goshen would hope for their favorite sons. He has a loving family, a thriving business, and he is giving back to the community. It's a good, if not a heroic, life.

-- Digression about use and the meaning of Hero --

Please take a moment, stop and think of a couple of your heroes. Doesn't matter whether you're picturing a mythological hero, someone of historical significance, a personal hero you encountered in your own life, or a comic-book superhero. Why is this person/creature your hero? What qualities makes her/him a hero to you? Does he or she inspire you to want to be a better person, to try to emulate the qualities, virtues, or values your hero stands for?

Television news-anchors have a tendency to refer to everyone in the US military, police officers, and firefighters as a Hero. Even more perversely, they conflate surviving victims of terror strikes with Hero. On this and other topics there is much drivel which emerges from the mouths of the lovely-coiffed and well-paid happy-talkers serving us on local-TV news-desks. Using *hero* in such an unrestrained fashion trivializes the term. The definition given in Google Dictionary reprinted at the beginning of the book provides the various uses the term has in serious conversation.

An example of the trivialization of *hero*: Summing up a human interest piece at the end of an evening network newscast about nurses, the anchorman enthused, "Nurses, our American heroes!" The story was not about nurses saving lives at the risk of their own. It was a very sweet little piece about a retired nurse being cared for by a young woman the retired nurse had cared for when the young nurse had been a little girl with a serious medical condition. It was a parable of "what comes around goes around" with a positive twist.

The two featured nurses had performed their professional craft with dedication. Nurses in the ER, ICU, surgical units, and other positions save lives, heal, and prolong life every day. That is their job. Some undoubtedly go above and beyond the call of duty. We even call extreme efforts taken by physicians and nurses to keep a patient alive who would otherwise die "heroic measures". Some nurses are heroes. But to imply that all nurses are American heroes deflates the meaning of the term.

Google Dictionary: *Hero: A person, typically a man, who is admired or idealized for courage, outstanding achievements, or noble qualities. Synonyms: brave person, brave man/woman, man/woman of courage, man/woman of the hour, lionheart, warrior, knight; champion, victor, conqueror.*

To call someone a hero should not be inconsequential. Being a hero means something quite different than doing a good job, surviving trauma, and/or helping others. A hero is extraordinary, a lionheart who is admired or idealized for outstanding achievements or noble qualities.

A delightful little essay in **The American Scholar**, Spring 2016, by Mark Edmundson, entitled "Off to See the Wizard", argues that a hero is more than lionhearted. Dorothy in *The Wizard of Oz* becomes the hero in the story as she grows into and displays the virtues her three companions wish to acquire. Cowardly Lion seeks to find Courage. The Tin Man wants to gain Wisdom. Scarecrow just wants a heart, which represents Compassion. Edmundson claims that these "are the three primary ideals of the ancient world."

Ideals remind us that there is more to life than serving ourselves. They offer us the chance to do something for others. Ideals also promise unity and focus and the chance to live fully in the present. ... When you've acquired some guts and brains and heart, you can make a little luck for yourself. Then all good things become possible, including the defeat of a wicked witch or any other worrisome antagonist who might cross your path. (Edmundson, p. 17)

Heroes are extraordinary because they embody and reveal to the rest of us the ideals we should strive to live by. "You can learn about courage from Homer, wisdom from Plato, and compassion from Jesus of Nazareth -- and also from Confucius and Buddha." (Edmundson, p. 16)

Let's not contribute to the trivialization of *hero*, when we think about and decide who our heroes should be. They should inspire us to become braver, wiser, and more compassionate.

By the late 1980s, when Rick Mirer was beginning to win football games for Goshen High, John Ritter had faded into the cobwebs of my youthful memories. I was married, had two little boys, a house with a two-car garage and mortgage, and a busy law practice. I wondered now and then about what had become of my childhood hero. I recall hearing rumors passed on by Goshen friends that Ritter had lost his job at Eli Lilly Co., gotten divorced, and had a drinking problem. There was even talk that he had gambling debts and a drug problem, and he'd left Lilly in disgrace. I discounted most of these rumors as sensationalism. If John Ritter was not going to live up to our expectations by starring in the NBA, he could at least serve as grist for the rumor mill. A fallen hero was a better story than that he'd faded into grey corporate obscurity.

    I never saw John Ritter back in Goshen after he graduated from IU. My boys never got his autograph. They grew up in Indianapolis knowing nothing of John Ritter's excellence as an athlete and person. At my urging, they did read a couple of my Chip Hilton books that had survived our moves and avoided the dumpster. John supposedly still lived in Indianapolis, but I never encountered him or tried to look him up.

    Every once in awhile I'd witness a particularly graceful play in a basketball game, and a visual memory of John Ritter's elegance might pop into mind. And then, I'd remind myself of that moment when I was nine and felt blessed by John Ritter's compliment.

Chapter Nine

Fallen Hero

In 1995 a friend and client of mine, Phil (not his real name), flagged down a cab outside the Indianapolis Airport for the drive home after his return flight on a business trip. The cab driver was a huge bald man. The cabbie looked like he weighed three hundred pounds. Phil noticed the cabbie's name was John Ritter.

Phil played high school basketball at one of the South Bend schools and at a small Indiana college. He is a few years older than John and never played against him. But, being a life-long IU fan from Northern Indiana, Phil had followed Ritter's high school and college careers. Phil judged John Ritter to be one of the best and most versatile basketball players he's ever seen play the game with "almost perfect shooting form".

Phil took a chance and asked the cabbie whether he'd played basketball. Indeed, he had, because it was that John Ritter.

In a long conversation during the drive from the airport to Phil's home in a suburb north of Indianapolis, John related to Phil how his life had spiraled downward. Phil passed on to me a sad tale of job losses, divorce, depression, a drinking problem, and homelessness.

Phil called on John to drive him a couple more times in the following months. On one of the occasions he hired John they played HORSE in Phil's driveway. He beat John one out of two games. I would have deemed Phil's claim a "fisherman's tale" but for his description of John's physical condition.

John told Phil that he "had to drive a cab or die." Phil also said that John looked older than his years. "John had sadness but also kindness in his eyes."

A Goshen acquaintance, who played on summer league baseball teams with John, described an encounter he had with John. "Roger" thinks it was in 1989 or 1990. (The timing is inconsistent with the year given by John in an interview, quoted in Chapter Fifteen, in which he stated that he quit his last corporate job in 1991, but Roger is confident the encounter was before that). Anyway, he told me that he chanced upon John in the lobby of a north-side Indianapolis hotel. Roger said that John must have parked his cab and was on his way to use the hotel's rest room, presumably as a personal grooming station. "John looked very scruffy. He needed a shower." Roger was shocked to see John in that condition.

Roger is a couple years older than John, but Roger told me he had always looked up to John. He had tremendous admiration for John's athletic ability, especially the accuracy of his pitching in baseball and shooting in basketball. But just as impressive was the way John had comported himself as a teammate. "John Ritter was one of my heroes," Roger confided.

John shook Roger's hand and gave him a wane smile, then made his way across the lobby to the Men's Room.

Another old friend of mine, who knows much of John's story through various connections with John, painted an even more miserable picture of John's fall from grace, which included gambling, drugs, and crime. He informed me that John had lost many of his teeth, which he surmised was a result of drug use and homelessness. I don't doubt the sincerity of this source, especially since I received similar information from two others, but the depth of misery portrayed reached a level of such appalling horror my sympathy for John Ritter forbids me to go any further with his description.

When I asked Coach Mirer whether he knew of John's troubles, he confirmed that he did and had tried to talk with John about his situation. Mirer said he didn't want to talk about these conversations with John, but wanted me to know that John made it clear he did not want to be pitied.

How could this have happened to the golden boy of Goshen? That beautiful form which glided so confidently and gracefully past opposing players to shoot a jump shot, dunk the ball, or grab a rebound. The Academic All-American. How was it possible that the best basketball player in the history of my hometown, and my childhood hero, had become a fat, bald, depressed cab driver with a drinking problem? Nothing against baldness or driving a cab -- lots of guys look great with a bald head and driving a cab is an honest living. But the picture Phil's description created in my mind of John in 1995, when he would have been 44 or 45, was so different than the image stored in my memory of the last time I had seen John on TV playing in the 1973 NCAA Tournament. Cognitive dissonance is too mild a term.

As a basketball player and high school role model, John Ritter seemed like he wholly inhabited himself, no mind/body dichotomy. By that I mean, when he played ball, it looked like John Ritter was in a flow state, where the mind and body are perfectly synced. A teammate of John's told me that he once saw John throw a pass the length of the basketball court -- behind his back! -- dead on target into the hands of a streaking teammate.

Walking the halls of Goshen High with his erect posture, easy gate, and boyish good looks, John Ritter looked and acted the part of the All-American boy. He truly was Goshen's finest. Twenty-two years after his last game as a college athlete, Phil's description evoked an image of a great lumbering hulk uncomfortable in his own skin. I tried to imagine a middle-aged John Ritter alienated from his own body, without friends, family, or a community. How could our Chip Hilton have turned into an obese, lonely, depressive cab driver? It was hard to imagine.

-- A cry for help rejected --

By sheer coincidence, around this same time frame in 1995, I met Bobby Knight. He was the keynote speaker at a father-son banquet at Second Presbyterian Church in Indianapolis. My nine year-old son James won one of the door prizes at the banquet. His prize was a crimson duffel bag with IU lettered in white on the side of the bag. James also received a pat on the head by Coach Knight of the IU Hoosiers. The huge bear of a man known for his terrible temper gently patted my little boy on the head and told James he expected to see him at IU in a few years.

Not long after meeting Knight, I was working on an article about coaching youth sports for a local publication, *Indy's Child*. I wanted to use a quote from the speech Coach Knight gave at the father-son banquet. (The quote was to the effect that kids should work on fundamental athletic skills, which would help develop their physical abilities, discipline, and character. The article and my copy of it are lost in the pre-digitized age. I still have a revised version of the article, which was published years later in another magazine, but I didn't use the Knight quote in the revised article. So, I can't remember or reprint the exact quote.) Anyway, I wrote Coach Knight a letter including the quote and asked if I got it right. My letter went on to tell him about what I had learned from Phil about John Ritter. I asked whether Knight might be able to extend a helping hand to his former star player.

I received a prompt reply from Coach Knight. He agreed that I had correctly captured his attitude about coaching youth sports and it was fine with him that I include the quote in the article. The letter went on to say that he had tried to stay in touch with Ritter and that John knew Coach Knight's door was always open to him. But John had not walked through it. (I clearly remember the door-metaphor Knight used, because it was surprisingly literary coming from someone with such a gruff public persona. I'm constrained from putting it in quotes, because I don't have the letter. Phil collects autographs, so I gave him the letter and stupidly did not keep a copy. Unfortunately, Phil lost the letter.)

    Phil's encounter with Ritter and my correspondence with Bob Knight occurred over twenty years ago as I'm writing this. I thought seriously about trying to locate John back in 1995. But I didn't. What did I have to say to him? I didn't have a job to offer him. What could I do for him? I had a family and a law business to take care of and my own life to live. I remember thinking about John and what he had meant to our hometown. I remember thinking he had been a flesh and blood Chip Hilton in my youthful mind. And, I remember wondering how John's life could have turned out so different from what his hometown fans expected. The picture in my mind of the John Ritter that had been a hero to my nine year-old self refused to sync up with the picture Phil's description evoked.

    But life moved on and time passed. Years later, in 2015, I connected on Facebook with an acquaintance from Goshen who had been a classmate of John's. We met for coffee. Dean (not his real name) related to me a sad and disappointing incident about John and Goshen. Dean's father was a Goshen businessman who had been very active in the local Chamber of Commerce for many years. According to Dean's dad, after John lost his job with Lilly, John came up to Goshen and asked the Chamber of Commerce to find him a job. He was rebuffed.

    I couldn't understand that. It made no sense to me that the local business community wouldn't welcome back home with open arms the man who'd been the most famous face of the Goshen Redskins. Dean's response: "Because by then John had become a huge drunk!"

    I guess the answer to my question of what did John Ritter get out of sticking and being "true to his school" (as the Beach Boys sang when we were kids) was -- not a damn thing! When he was in need, the town, through the powers that be in the business community, turned its collective back on him. That's a hard one to accept. Dean's father passed away years ago, so that source is not available. But Dean was adamant that he clearly remembered what his father told him.

I always thought of Goshen as a caring community; a place where everyone knows your name. If you were from the right side of the tracks, and certainly for our star athletes, the town's establishment would bend over backwards to help you out in a time of need. Guess not in the 1990s.

When I was growing up in Goshen, the willingness to take care of our own was so strong that the town even created the job of guarding the city dump for a brain-damaged member of the community. In the early 1960s, when you drove your car or truck in to the city dump to drop off excess trash, "Two Gun Johnny" (because he dressed like a cowboy with two toy-guns holstered on his belt) would be standing at the entrance. He made sure you paid the quarter for the privilege of using the dump.

The willingness to take care of our own was even more apparent for the children of families of privilege and athletes. For those within the right social circle, if your kid got into trouble with the law, so long as it wasn't too serious, it would be handled discretely. Officer Hess would pay a visit to your house to make sure your parents were meting out appropriate discipline. No need to bring actual charges and create a record that might have untoward consequences for one of our young people. (Yes, I know this from personal experience. I also know from personal experience that this brand of informal justice applied to kids from the other side of the tracks who were athletes.)

So why, when John Ritter, who had given so much of his sweat to kindle pride in our town, did the Chamber of Commerce turn its back on him? Just because he had a drinking problem? Hell, when I was growing up many of the businessmen in town drank like Don Draper in *Madmen*.

On the other hand, there is a cruel symmetry to this part of the story, if John had, indeed, turned in members of the high school baseball team for drinking and going to a strip club, and then three decades later John was turned away by the Goshen establishment for a drinking problem.

-- Self destruction --

Dean told me about an encounter he had with John that made John's rejection by the town even more painful to contemplate. Dean thinks it was in 2001 that he saw John scalping tickets at Deer Creek (an outdoor rock-concert venue northeast of Indianapolis). Dean was dropping off his daughter at a concert. Dean rolled the window down and called out, "John! How are you?" John's response: "I'm not John Ritter anymore." He turned his large back and lumbered off into the darkness.

Something Stu Swartz (retired **Goshen News** sports editor) had passed on to me, when I contacted him to ask about information on Ritter, began to make more sense. Stu messaged me through Facebook that he hoped I'd contact John and ask him to reconnect with Goshen. Stu informed me that John had been invited to join the Elkhart County Sports Hall of Fame, but John had refused to participate. Coach Mirer told me John is voted number one on the ballot for the Sports Hall of Fame every year, but John always turns it down "probably because he's embarrassed to come back to Goshen." I learned from other sources that John had not attended his high school class reunions. I could now well understand why John didn't want to return to Goshen.

The community had rejected John, and John was no longer John Ritter.

-- Leveling off from a tailspin? --

Contemplating the trajectory of John Ritter's life after graduation from IU made more poignant my memory of him patting me on the back when I was nine years-old and he was eleven or twelve. By 1995 my oldest son was nine. He had a younger brother, and we had a loving family, a nice house on the banks of the White River, and our lives were good. I thought about John Ritter, over-weight, bald, driving a cab, struggling with a drinking problem, and sometimes homeless. My heart ached, but I did nothing.

Ten years later in 2005 I saw an article in the **Indianapolis Star** referencing John. Since the **Star's** article (unlike mine in **Indy's Child**) is digitally archived, I can accurately quote it:

November 27, 2005,The Indianapolis Star from Indianapolis, Indiana, Page A15: ... The last resort for brokers is taking unsold tickets to the street, a scene that in Indianapolis often includes former Indiana University basketball player John Ritter, a Circle City Tickets employee. He stands out. "I'm 6-5,completely bald and older than most of them," said Ritter, who is 54. An academic All-American in 1973 under coach Bob Knight, Ritter said a divorce and depression sent his life into a tailspin. About 10 years ago, he met Harrison (owner or Circle City Tickets) at a game and started working in the ticket business. For street sellers who aren't connected to a broker, business is simpler, faster. Show up a few hours before the game. Try to buy tickets that a seller wants to unload quickly, at a below-market price. Try to sell higher. During his time in the business, Ritter said the number of street sellers has increased vastly. (parenthetical added)

The quote is from an article about ticket brokers and scalpers in Indianapolis and their relationship to the professional sports teams in town. It goes on to describe how difficult the life of a ticket scalper is. It's a boom or bust business. If there is sufficient excitement about a team so that games sell out and tickets are in demand, a broker can sell tickets at a premium. If the team is in the doldrums, the broker might take a bath and have to sell tickets at a loss.

I remember reading the article in 2005. That was ten years after Phil told me about his cab ride with John and my correspondence with Coach Knight. By 2005 Bob Knight had left IU in disgrace. My connections with the old hometown,

Goshen, were tenuous. I no longer had any family living there. My parents and my brother's family had moved south to Florida by then. I attended high school class reunions, but otherwise contacts with friends still living in Goshen were infrequent. (Facebook and other connective social media were not yet available to the masses.) My life was still fully engaged as husband, father (my oldest would graduate from high school in 2005), and partner in a small downtown law firm.

I wondered then what John's life at age 54 was like. The article confirmed much of what Phil had related; there had been a divorce, depression, and John had gone into a "tailspin". But how was he doing now, ten years down the road since he'd driven Phil home from the airport in 1995? Was he pulling himself out of the tailspin? The *Indianapolis Star* article indicated that John had been "working in the ticket business" for "about 10 years". I surmised that he must have quit driving a cab and started trying to make a living scalping tickets not long after his encounter with Phil and my correspondence with Bob Knight. Was there a connection? Had some undercurrent of Fate lifted John out of a desperate situation into a somewhat better one?

In the Internet search I conducted for this writing project to find articles mentioning John, I came across a eulogy in the *Elkhart Truth* newspaper for John's high school coach, Art Cosgrove, who died in 2005 at the age of 92. John is quoted extensively in the March 30, 2005 article. His remarks in tribute to Coach Cosgrove are kind, respectful, and appropriate. For example, "He was like a second father to a lot of us that played for him." John expressed disappointment "that we did not win the semistate" for Coach Cosgrove, and that no team coached by Cosgrove made it to a state championship. John's younger brother Mike is the one other player of Coach Cosgrove's quoted in the article.

John's record-setting play in high school and college are related in the article, but no mention is made of John's personal history post-IU graduation. The *Elkhart Truth* article was silent about John's current situation in 2005, and did not even report where he lived. The reporter did relate that brother Mike had followed Cosgrove into the coaching profession and had been an assistant basketball coach at Goshen and head coach at Fremont High School.

    Was John embarrassed to disclose his occupation as a ticket scalper, or did the reporter think it irrelevant? John does not come across in the article as someone who has been homeless, depressed, or struggling with any serious issues. John provided a sophisticated description of Coach Cosgrove's offensive strategy, which is quoted in full near the end of the article. Had any Ritter fans unaware of John's torturous life journey read the article in 2005, I think the response would have been: Yup, that's our guy; still as decent, bright, thoughtful, and into basketball as ever.

    The 2005 *Indianapolis Star* article described John as an "employee" of Circle City Tickets. That implied a regular job. Being an employee of a ticket broker was surely a better situation than just trying to scalp tickets on his own. John's clarity in the Cosgrove eulogy, and that he had regular employment, was evidence that he had climbed out of the pit he'd fallen into after his divorce. By 2005 he was no longer a homeless cabbie.

    Still, I made no effort to contact my former hero.

Chapter Ten

Rejected

The next time I remember talking about John Ritter was on October 19, 2012 at the JW Marriott Hotel in Indianapolis at a banquet to celebrate the 75th Anniversary of Marian University's incarnation in Indianapolis. Marian traces its roots back to a log cabin school in Oldenburg, Indiana, which was started in 1851 by a nun from the Order of the Sisters of St. Francis. Her mission was to teach the German-speaking children of southeastern Indiana. By 1937 the school had become an accredited college and moved to the state capitol, Indianapolis. By 2009 it had grown into a university.

The 75th anniversary celebration was quite a gala event with musical entertainment, cheerleaders, singing nuns, steak dinner, and hobnobbing with big donors to the university. I was a guest of a friend who is one of the bigwig donors. "Jim" had helped make arrangements with the university for me to teach a class about philanthropy and then lead an international-study tour in Nepal during the spring term of 2013.

Steve Downing, John Ritter's teammate at IU, had just been hired as the Athletic Director at Marian in May of 2012. Towering over all the other guests at six foot eight, Downing was easy to spot at the dinner gala. I asked Jim to introduce me.

-- *Three All-Stars* --

So this was where Steve Downing's life journey had brought him. Downing and his teammate at Washington High School, George McGinnis, and John Ritter were the three Indiana High School All-Stars of the Class of 1969 recruited by

Coach Lou Watson to restore Indiana University Basketball to greatness. The incredible strength of McGinnis and Downing, both of whom were six foot eight inches tall and weighed almost 240 pounds as nineteen-year old sophomores, would be the twin towers to dominate the boards and provide unmatched inside scoring. Ritter would add finesse and outside sharpshooting. The triumvirate was expected to be the foundation of the next Hoosier basketball dynasty. But, as we know, the Hoosiers imploded that first year McGinnis, Downing, and Ritter donned their Cream and Crimson pinstriped warm-ups.

Seems that life, nevertheless, turned out pretty well for two of the three high school All-Stars. George McGinnis did set records the one year he played at IU. In the 1970-71 season Big George became the first sophomore to lead the Big Ten in scoring and rebounding. He averaged 29.9 points per game and was named an All-American and earned All-Big Ten Honors. He left college to play pro ball after the tumultuous year ending with Watson's resignation.

George was drafted by the Indiana Pacers, which had become a dominant team in the young American Basketball Association. McGinnis won ABA championships with the Pacers and was a perennial All-Star. "Big Mac" was the ABA Co-Most Valuable Player with the great Dr. J, Julius Erving, in 1975. George scored more points that year than Dr. J, leading the league in scoring. After the ABA merged with the NBA, McGinnis played on three different teams but spent the beginning and end of his career with his hometown Pacers.

The Pacers reacquired McGinnis near the end of his playing days in the hopes that he would add leadership and a spark to a struggling team. They traded a young player named Alex English for George. Watching Big George play for the Indiana Pacers at the end of his career left his hometown fans in anguish. He still had incredible strength and speed for a man of his size, but he'd lost his touch with the basketball. His shooting percentage was miserable. Alex English went on to become one of the most prolific scorers in NBA history. The trade was popular with Pacer fans at the time, but turned out to be one of the worst transactions ever made in the NBA. Still, Big George was a three-time All-Star in the NBA. His jersey, Number 30, was retired by the Pacers and still hangs majestically in Bankers Life Fieldhouse, the Pacers' current home.

After his pro career ended, George McGinnis became a successful businessman, local philanthropist, and is still a popular figure at Indianapolis sporting and cultural events.

Steve Downing followed a different path to achieve worldly success. Like Ritter, he graduated from IU in 1973. He and John were co-captains of the Hoosiers their senior year under Bobby Knight. That was the season which really launched Bob Knight's rise to fame as a college basketball coach (and later infamy due to his out-of-control violence visited upon players, staff, referees, and finally an IU student).

Steve and John's senior year was the year that IU made it to the NCAA semi-final game losing to John Wooden's UCLA Bruins. The Hoosiers lost the game, but Downing outplayed and scored more points than the great Bill Walton.

The Hoosiers played from behind the whole game, but closed within two points. It was beginning to look like the underdog Hoosiers might pull off a major upset. And then, Downing fouled out. Hoosier fans have argued the call ever since, claiming Walton charged Downing. Both centers had four fouls, so whichever player drew the whistle was out of the game. If Walton had been bounced, IU might have won. After IU lost Steve's fearsome rebounding and inside scoring, they fell further and further behind for a final score of 59 to 70.

Downing won the Chicago Tribune Silver Basketball award in 1973 as the best player in the Big Ten Conference. At the end of the season he was selected as the 17th pick in the NBA draft by the Boston Celtics with the team's first pick.

Downing only played one full season with the Celtics, although it was a pretty good year to be on the team. They won the NBA Championship with cigar-chomping Red Auerbach as General Manager and Team Captain John Havlicek. Steve was waived by the Celtics after three games in the 1974-75 season. No other NBA team picked him up. At six foot eight inches he was really too short to play center against the 7-footers in the NBA. But there was another problem -- Steve was too nice. A fan website, *Celtics Life*, features an article entitled, "What the Hell Happened to...Steve Downing?" The article cites several sources, including Celtics teammates, that describe Steve as placid, sheepish, and not mentally tough enough for the NBA. He'd been a monster on the court for IU, but shrunk into a klutzy puppy with the Celtics.

I don't know how Steve Downing reacted to being cut by the Boston Celtics at the very beginning of his second season as a pro. The records I can find indicate that he must have given up on professional basketball. I haven't found any record of him playing on any other team or in another league. Maybe it was a relief to get cut by the Celtics for a guy that is described as too nice for the NBA.

Steve found another route to success within athletics. He came back to Indiana as an employee in the IU Athletic Department. He moved on to a better position at Texas Tech University, where he spent ten years as senior associate director of athletics. The capstone of his career is likely his current one as head of Marian University's Athletic Department. It's a small school but Marian is a powerhouse in athletics. It's won multiple national championships in bicycling and has recently won championships in football and women's' basketball. Steve Downing has a nice little empire to rule with his gentle touch.

-- *Reconnecting* --

After my introduction to Downing at the 75th Gala Celebration in 2012, we engaged in the kind of forced bonhomie typical of grown men meeting each other for the first time. I told Steve I was from Goshen and an old friend of John Ritter's. (That was a stretch, well, maybe it even qualifies as a white lie. Given my very limited actual contact with John Ritter, I certainly didn't qualify as a friend.) Steve warmed up and became genuinely friendly at the mention of his college teammate. He told me that he had been in touch with John and could give me his phone number, if I wanted it. He gave me his new business card as Marian's Athletic Director, and said to call or email him to remind him to give me John's number.

    I sent Steve an email a week later and received a prompt reply from his assistant with John's phone number. I didn't call it.

    Three years later in 2015 I was feeling the urge to take on a new writing project. I'd finished my last book a year ago and was truly sick and tired of spending time doing the marketing and social media expected of authors. The itch to write and my nagging curiosity about what had become of John Ritter, and why his life had taken a course so different than what I would have predicted, converged. I'd saved the phone number Steve Downing gave me in 2012. After screwing up my courage, I called it. A recording informed me it was no longer in service.

    Steve had said that John worked for Circle City Tickets (as the 2005 **Indianapolis Star** article about ticket scalping reported). So, not to be deterred, I took a deep breath and called Circle City Tickets. I asked for John Ritter.

    Hs voice was almost exactly as I remembered it, although slightly deeper. It had the sound of polite intelligence. There was firmness yet a gentleness in John's voice. It surprised me that he knew who I was. Why would he? But there was no inauthenticiy or a false tone detectable. He didn't try to sell me any tickets. His voice conveyed genuine warmth and mild curiosity.

I told John I was interested in writing about him. There was a pause, then he said he didn't understand why I would want to do that. I explained that I wanted to explore with him how his life had been as the golden boy of our high school and how life had gone for him since then. There was a longer pause. He expressed skepticism that anyone would be interested in him. I disagreed. Said I understood he'd had some hard times and that the arc of his life was somewhat like a Greek tragedy. But, he must be doing okay now and people could learn from that.

John remained polite, curious, and skeptical throughout the conversation. I told him that I envisioned spending several sessions interviewing and recording him. John said he'd like to think about it for a week and then we could talk again. He gave me his cell phone number.

About a week later I received a text thanking me for my interest but that he declined. I called back, but didn't reach John. I received a voicemail which was apologetic and explained that he had children and grandchildren and he didn't want to reveal things they didn't need to know about his life.

I persisted, and reached him on the phone again. I urged John to reconsider. But he said that, if his story was going to be told, the whole truth would need to come out and he just didn't think that would be good for his kids and grandkids. I tried to persuade him by saying that his story would be valuable to people who wanted to experience fame as an athlete, or in any field, and he could offer advice about how to cope with success and failure. And, despite the troubles he'd had, he had come through it. His story was ultimately one of triumph over tragedy. John said he'd like to think it over and he'd call me back in a week.

After a couple weeks I received a voicemail in which John said he really appreciated the work I'd done and he was sorry to disappoint me, but he could not agree to be interviewed for an article or a book about him. It wouldn't be good for his family, and that had to be his first concern.

    I reached him by phone again and asked if I could take him out to dinner or lunch and chat some more about my ideas for the writing project about him. I assured him that we wouldn't have to go into any details that he didn't want revealed to his children and grandchildren. John thanked me again, apologized again, but said unless we told the whole story it wouldn't be worth doing and he just wasn't willing to risk any adverse effect on his children and their children.

    Well, what the hell. Maybe it was a stupid idea. I was leaving for a trip out West with my wife and a visit with our son, Andrew, in Los Angeles. It wasn't the right time to begin a new writing project anyway. So, I ditched the whole idea.

Part Three

Reconsideration

Chapter Eleven

Humanity of a Hero

-- Heroes inspire stories --

What was I thinking anyway? My childish reminiscences about my fictional sports hero and his real life embodiment didn't have enough traction to become a full-length book. Who would want to read about John Ritter other than a few middle-aged and elderly fans from the Goshen area that remember John's glory days playing for the Goshen Redskins. (Some readers might even be turned off by our hometown's team name. But then, lo and behold, the name was changed. After a year of contentious debate with pressure from community residents concerned about sensitivity to Native Americans and resistance from die-hard traditionalists, the Goshen School Board decided in the Fall of 2015 to change the team name from Redskins to RedHawks as of January 1, 2016. But we're stuck with "Goshen Redskins", like it, or not like it, when referring to the team during John's and my era.)

Rabid fans of "IU Nation" might be curious to learn what's become of a former Hoosier great. However, few would be interested in slogging through a full-length book about John Ritter and the musings of a retired lawyer turned writer and cracker barrel philosopher. If the subject was about the actor John Ritter, there might be a broader market. That John Ritter was a Hollywood celebrity. (When you Google search "John Ritter", a lot more entries turn up about the actor than the basketball player. I've learned the actor was a fine human being who died too young. His life seems like it was short and mostly sweet, unlike Goshen's John Ritter, who has lived longer but had a long stretch lacking any sweetness.)

    Maybe John was right in his initial response to my query -- that nobody would want to read about him. But here we are, and I think, and hope you, friendly reader, will agree there is more to consider than just the life of John Ritter, a high school and college basketball star that didn't make it in the pros and then fell onto hard times.

    This is not just a biography of John Ritter. I have not set out to meticulously discover, verify, and present the results of prodigious research about my childhood hero. There are statements herein that might diverge widely from what others remember and how they would characterize John. John might disagree with some of what I have written, and he would probably prefer certain portions were not published. Members of John's family may have a completely different take on John's life journey.

    This project is as much memoir as biography. It fits under the literary genre of "creative nonfiction", because I am trying to create a story, using memories and research and imagination, which was inspired by wondering about what happened to John Ritter after his glory days as a basketball star ended. Why wonder about him and how his life has turned out other than idle curiosity?

    John Ritter is of particular interest not because he was an old friend I'd lost touch with. I didn't really know John personally. I wondered about John Ritter, because, like Chip Hilton, memorable images of him were imprinted in my childhood consciousness under "Hero". And, despite everything I've learned about the "tailspin" of John's life, he still fits in that file.

Other kids around my age in the Goshen area surely looked up to John Ritter as I did. I'm sure I'm not the only one in whose mind John's image took root as the prototypical sports hero. Imagistic memories of John Ritter are embedded in the consciousness of older basketball fans too. Phil, Dean, Roger, Tad, and other contemporaries of John I've spoken with all carry vivid memories of John as an Indiana sports icon as long as I have. I've spoken with people from Goshen in their eighties who would like to know what's become of John, because they remember his exceptional ability on the basketball court and that he was such a remarkably fine young man.

At a second encounter with Steve Downing, he said of John, "He was the smartest one of all of us (referring to his IU teammates). He was a brilliant guy." He shook his head and added, "It's just a shame what happened to him. What a shame."

Over breakfast with a married couple from Goshen, who were contemporaries of John, the wife confessed that talking about what's happened to John Ritter, "brings tears to my eyes." Her husband agreed, but said John should still be considered a hero in Goshen and to IU fans. "John's talent was spectacular. He's one of a kind."

John Ritter was unique for our town. He made a profound impression on many who knew him, and many who only knew of him. So, to me, and to others who witnessed his athletic heroics and were aware of his academic prowess and extreme commitment to personal virtue, John Ritter is more than just a curiosity. He is the protagonist of a story about the golden boy of Goshen, Indiana, our Chip Hilton. The story I have learned is worth telling, because it is a story of an extraordinary life journey.

The deep psychology of the Hero archetype unmoors the representative character from historical facts. For those of us who admired John Ritter when he was in the public eye, the statistics he racked up on basketball courts may have drifted out of our active memories. But his image as an athlete who played with uncommon grace and behaved with unusual personal virtue off the court lingers. John Ritter was exceptional in the way he personified the ideal boy, teenager, and young man of a bygone era. Like his fictional doppelganger, Chip Hilton, John represented an ideal type in the collective consciousness of many who knew of him in Goshen and at Indiana University. John was a basketball star in the late 1960s and early 70s, but the ideal he represents was established in the 1950s. He resides in the minds of those who "knew" him as an example of that Chip Hilton-like archetypal sports hero.

Archetypal heroes and their deeds are the stuff of stories. We like to remember and tell the stories of the great ones, their victories and conquests, their sidekicks and comrades. In some cases, the appeal grows as that type of hero is rarely seen in real life any longer. The straight-arrow sports star, who speaks humbly and dresses plainly, has retreated from popular culture. Brashness and bling, or intentional nerd-geek style, are de rigueur for today's stars. Sports heroes and pop stars of the Chip Hilton old-school variety are fading from memory. You might still see them on Turner Classic Movies and grainy documentaries, but rarely on live TV or in real life. (Even white high school athletes from small towns in Indiana wear baggy saggies and make gang gestures at the camera.) So, I am creating a story about a sort of hero that many of us still admire, but is heading toward extinction.

Telling a story is to carry on the ancient tradition of the community sitting around a fire. As the wood burns and flames begin to dance and sway and sparks crackle and are spit out of the fire pit, the story-teller's voice begins to rise. The story is inspired by a hero of long ago, or by one among us, and by deeds that might have been done but probably exaggerated for greater effect. As the story is spun out a narrative develops which connects the community with its past and present. Through the shared experience of hearing about the glorious triumphs and poignant travails of the hero the village bonds are strengthened.

Facts are not immaterial, but are secondary.

Just as we cannot reconstruct exact personal memories, we cannot construct exact historical memories. We must fill in the details with educated speculations. But that's okay, because if factual errors result from the impulse to construct a sincere and just historical narrative -- a narrative that inspires true insight, and maybe even the better angels of our nature -- then the payoff can take us further than factual accuracy ever could (even if it were achievable). Wisdom thus derives not only from formal history but also from more open imaginative reconstructions of the past. (McWilliams, p. 29)

As McWilliams urges in his ***American Scholar*** article, my aspiration is to create a narrative of "collective memory" which "can take us beyond ourselves and into a relationship with others, bound by a shared story -- a story that's created to serve higher purposes than mere truth." (McWilliams, p. 30)

My mind has now accessed the memory of John Ritter patting me on the back, when I was nine, so many times, I wonder how much that memory has changed in the chemistry of my neural circuitry. Did it even happen? It is crystal clear in my mind. But so is my memory of Mary Hilton at the company ball.

Does it matter whether John actually congratulated me on playing a great game at Rogers Park in 1962? To an extent, yes; but on another level, not really. The incident, whatever was its now unreachable reality, is an inspiration "to serve higher purposes than mere truth." It has inspired the questions we are considering about what it means to be a hero.

-- Human being or abstraction? --

When the story is about a real and existing person there

is an obligation of fairness and decency in how we treat her. While they are still alive and have their own feelings and consciousness, heroes are not *just* archetypes or ideals in our minds. They are also human. What do we owe living characters that get deeply embedded in our own psyche?

The memories which we hang on to from childhood help to create who we are as we move on through the other life stages of human development. Some philosophers, poets, and pundits tell us that we are our memories. What meaning would there be to life if it was lived solely in the present or thinking only about the future without a past? We would be different people, in terms of personality, self-understanding, and character, if our memories were different.

We are created by relationships and encounters we have through direct experience with others which are preserved in memory. But not all meaningful relationships and encounters are with others through direct experience. Some are through stories. In our culture we experience story via many different media. We encounter and develop relationships in our minds and hearts with fictional and historical characters, as well as living persons, through TV shows, movies, radio, books, and other means which have replaced the communal gathering around the fire pit. But still, the characters we encounter that we care about come to inhabit our minds. The ones that stay with us become guides and standards of comparison. ["Wow! Josh is as big and strong as The Hulk." "I'm in love! Emma is as beautiful as Helen of Troy." "That bastard! Dan is two-faced as Iago." "What an idiot! Steve is about as stupid as Jim Carey in *Dumb and Dumber*."]

The characters that stay with us, whether as Hero, Villain, Sage, Trickster, Lover, or Goofball, get filed under categories -- archetypes --within our minds. They are a valuable resource. They build and refine our knowledge base about what it means to be Stupid, Tricky, Erotic, Wise, Courageous, Compassionate, etc. We are in debt to these characters (and the creators of the fictional ones). But, what are the consequences for a nonfictional actual-human-being when others think so highly of him that he becomes a Hero? What is left of the humanity of a local hero, when she becomes a character in stories and grist for the rumor mill?

    The first time I started writing this sentence in the Fall of 2015 I had not spoken to John Ritter since he turned me down for a dinner date a few months earlier. But I did speak with John again in February 2016, after I finished the first draft of this book. I asked if he would like to see the manuscript before it was submitted for publication. He thanked me and declined. He said he would read it after publication. I didn't ask, and John didn't tell me anything of substance about his life in our phone conversations. I have not spoken with John's ex-wife, any of his children, or his brother Mike to get their input about John's life journey. Out of deference to John's concerns about not exposing his family to "things they don't need to know", they are, for the most part, left out of the story I am telling about John Ritter.

    It may seem odd, but the John Ritter character that has developed in my imagination, since I began seeking to solve the mystery of what happened to him after IU graduation, has come to feel closer to me, and more real, than many people I see on a regular basis and call "friend".

    As I learned more about John's life through research on the Internet, from communications with people who have known and cared about John, and simply pondering his life as a story, a more fully fleshed out character began to emerge in my mind and heart than the John Ritter I had admired in my youthful innocence, more fully developed than John Ritter the cab driver I was shocked to learn about from Phil. He is no longer just an old and dusty memory. Nor is he an idol up on a pedestal.

    More than a few nights during the writing process of this book I awoke worrying about John. The image of him alone in his cab haunted me. Writing was the release from obsessively imagining how he coped with the tribulations he'd suffered through. It was a torment to think about how differently John must have felt about himself from when he was the hometown hero to lonely nights sleeping in his cab. As one old friend of John's confided, "It makes me cry thinking about what John has gone through."

It comes out sounding a bit weird to care about someone deeply that I don't really know in a close personal relationship. But all of the old friends and acquaintances of John Ritter with whom I've spoken think of John as special, as someone worthy of taking a special interest in.

John had (maybe still has) charisma, which comes from the Greek for *grace*. *Graceful* kept coming up in descriptions of John as an athlete, but also in the way he comported himself around others. Yes, he was operating on a different wavelength from his teammates when he was at odds with them, but he was still chosen as captain of every high school and college team on which he played. John's gracefulness and virtuousness left an impression on those who have known him.

A female friend of John's from high school described what a sweet and winsome guy he was around girls. "I would use the word gentleness rather than gracefulness," she said. "But compared to most of us at that time in our lives he clearly showed more integrity, restraint, and focus." He was the star of the high school and towered over us, but was so "scrupulous in his behavior" several high school and college peers describe John as shy and self-effacing. Rather than trying to draw attention to himself, as is so common in the selfie culture, "John could fade into the background at a social gathering," a classmate said.

Every Goshen and IU person with whom I talked to about John was especially interested to know what has become of him. They were eager to share their own experiences of his gracefulness, gentleness, or uniqueness.

John Ritter made an impression on those he encountered, and that impression has stayed with us. He is a real person to be cared for empathetically. Yet, he is also a representational figure of how boys and young men were supposed to be "back in the day".

I know John far more deeply now than I did when we were kids growing up in Goshen, Indiana, although, I have not seen him and only had a few phone conversations and exchanges of messages. In a way, I know him as an imaginary friend. Imaginary in the sense that, while I don't have contact with the human being, he is very much alive in my mind and heart. I have a mental construct of him and an emotional attachment to him. I have come to care about him, like I care about dear friends, and want him to have a good life and to be happy and content.

Reading Clair Bee's books as a child, I rooted for Chip to win every game, to find ways to help his mom out, and to outsmart the bad kids that tried to sabotage him. I wanted to jump in and tell that dang Fats Olsen, and his henchman Stinky Ferris, to leave Chip alone and quit trying to tear him down! You're just envious because Chip is better than you, darn it!

As I came to know John more deeply in my own head and heart by reading what I could find about him on the Internet, talking with old friends of his, and just thinking about him and feeling for him, I wanted to do the same for him -- to go back in time and convince the Cleveland Cavaliers or Pacers they should give him a real shot as a pro. I wanted to tell the Goshen Chamber of Commerce, You owe him! Give him a damn job!

Instead, I'm writing about him, when he asked me not to. (Although, to be legalistic about it, John did not ask me not to write about him -- please excuse the double negative -- he just declined to allow me to interview him. He did not sound surprised when I offered to send him a pre-publication copy of the manuscript. So, he must have realized I was going to write about him even without his assistance.) I might be doing the real John Ritter harm rather than helping him. I could be accused of doing something similar, or worse, to what I suspected John of in his ethical decisions with the baseball team incidents and in the way he related to (or, was unable to relate to) his Hoosier teammates: valuing an abstract idea over other human beings; not being sufficiently compassionate; caring more about achieving a goal than the human beings involved.

Don't like the sound of that.

I really do feel for John. I undertook this project, in part, to solve the mystery of what happened to John Ritter and to try to understand what it was like to be John Ritter. I wanted to share what I learned so that sympathetic readers would imagine what John had experienced in his life journey.

This is not a psycho-biography of John Ritter. I'm not qualified to write one. And, I haven't created a psych-profile for a professional to review. It is my intention to write about John from an empathetic perspective. I hope and think that John might find value in what I'm writing. I did not set out to discover whatever it is that John does not want his family to learn. I haven't contacted any of his family members. I offered him the opportunity to read and respond to the manuscript before publication.

But I am not writing about John Ritter just because I empathize with him. And, I am telling almost everything I have learned about John's downward spiral in order to tell the whole story I have learned, which includes, I suspect, some aspects of his life John did not want me to write about. So, the accusation that I am not treating John as a fellow human being, whose welfare should be my greatest concern, does have merit.

I am telling a story in which the character John Ritter is the hero-protagonist. In that role he isn't exactly human. Well, he is, but he isn't.

The story of John Ritter illustrates the points I am trying to make about what it means to be a hero and how we treat our heroes. When we idealize real people they lose their humanity. They are turned into idols that we worship and may later want to destroy. Heroes are transformed from conscious-feeling fellow homo sapiens into characters in our stories. The greatest hero-characters will become legends or even mythic characters. We might think we know them, but when they are idolized they become more like treasured memories, existing in our minds as archetypal characters, rather than living-breathing human beings with thoughts and feelings of their own.

It may be that John was not treated humanely by the Goshen Chamber of Commerce, because they couldn't deal with him as a human being. He had been an idol of the town. That was how the town wanted to preserve him. This "huge drunk" that asked for help finding a job was not the John Ritter the town wanted to preserve in its memory. John Ritter should stay in the high school record books and trophy case, in the town's collective memory as an Indiana All-Star -- that's where he belongs; not as some pathetic character in need of a job. The incarnation of John Ritter that presented himself to the Goshen Chamber of Commerce asking for help was too much a contrast to our idealized version to deal with.

Two Gun Johnny had always been damaged, so to give him a job guarding the city dump did not create cognitive dissonance. He was who he was, and he needed help, so the town found a compassionate and intelligent way to deal with "Two Gun". But John Ritter presented a different challenge to the town fathers.

When Phil related to me what he learned from John about his life and the state of his physical and emotional condition in 1995, what was my reaction? Shock; no way! And then, sadness, sympathy, and curiosity. But I can't claim that my initial reaction was compassion. I made no effort to extend a helping hand or even to try to contact John. It would have been easier to do so had John been an old friend rather than someone I had idolized in my childhood and early teen years. It was uncomfortable to contrast and compare memories of that graceful character with Phil's description of a sad, overweight, recovering alcoholic.

-- Heroes with feet of clay or cardboard characters --

It is uncomfortable to examine Jesus, George Washington, Lincoln, Gandhi, and King in the harsh light that the media shines on the warts and foibles of current politicians, celebrities, and star athletes. Sure, some writers, playwrights, and historians have tried to portray our legendary and mythical heroes as mere humans with feet of clay. Such unflattering portraits invariably draw fire from hostile critics defending our immortals.

You might recall the firestorm of protest and invective that was unleashed by the religious right against the 2000 release of the film *The Last Temptation of Christ*. Jesus was portrayed to have carnal feelings for Mary Magdalene, and he was afraid to die. To portray the Christ as fallible and merely human was intolerable to some Christians. A more extreme and despicable reaction was the 2015 mass murder of the **Charlie Hebdo** staff by Muslim jihadists, because the magazine had satirized the Prophet.

Negative characterizations of our pantheon of cultural heroes are usually ignored within the milieu of traditional culture. The bedtime stories told by parents to their children, the Bible stories told to kids in Sunday School classes, and the inspirational tales told by grade-school teachers, are largely unaffected by revisionary histories. The carpenters of our culture are more comfortable with un-nuanced narratives about our historical heroes.

Typically, the way our most cherished heroes are represented, especially to the young, is that they are cardboard characters that stand for something. Whether it's

Lancelot or Lincoln, the Hero is portrayed in text books and popular media as above and beyond the rest of us ordinary folk.

Sir Lancelot is a fascinating and troubling character in the sagas of King Arthur's Round Table. He has been portrayed in various ways, but as an archetypal hero Lancelot represents Courage, Chivalry, and Male Beauty. As the betrayer of his liege lord by committing adultery with Queen Guinevere, Lancelot is the anti-hero Deceiver representing Infidelity.

Abraham Lincoln was a flesh and blood human being living his own life during a particular time. But after his assassination he became an icon. He became Honest Abe, a representational figure to school children for the value of Honesty/Truthfulness. Lincoln as historical martyr to the causes of Emancipation and Preservation of the Union stands for Equality, Reconciliation, and Compassion.

Dead heroes, just like fictional ones, become characters in the stories we tell to promote positive values within our communities. We use them to enculturate our young people.

Those who become heroes while living their own lives, but on whom we imprint ideals and principles, must then bear the burden of our expectations. They are expected to be living embodiments of ideals and principles. If they fail to live up to our expectations, well, woe be unto them.

I don't know whether it came naturally to John Ritter to behave like the perfect boy, whether it was a role he intentionally adopted, or whether he felt pressured into playing that role. The evidence from his peers is ambiguous. "That's just who John was," several different people who knew John when he was growing up remarked about him in our conversations. But, if being the perfect kid came so naturally to John, then why wasn't he truly close to teammates and classmates? Why was he "kind of shy, especially around girls," as every friend of his felt compelled to mention in describing what John was like as a teenager? I'm not sure John was entirely comfortable in his own skin as the perfect boy.

I think John Ritter was a person who lived by an extraordinarily high standard of personal integrity and felt pressured internally not to allow himself opportunities to deviate from the high road he'd chosen. His hometown and IU fans came to expect John to live up to our expectations that he would always be that ideal boy I saw in him through my 9-year old eyes. We put him on a pedestal, and woe unto John Ritter when he fell off it.

John seemed like the prototypical good-guy sports hero to his hometown fans, who would not let us down on or off the court. And so, we came to expect him to live up to our idealized version of that character. He did, for a third of a lifetime. When he could no longer stand to live under that pressure, he let us down and ceased to be that John Ritter.

I abstracted John Ritter from his humanity, when I idolized him as an innocent child, and I am guilty as charged for using him again within these pages as a character in a story I'm telling. Once again, John is being objectified by my equating him with other archetypal heroes. My excuse is that by telling the story of what John Ritter has meant to me, we will learn something about how a real person gets elevated from ordinary life onto the pedestal of Hero. And, we can consider the consequences both for the hero and for those who elevated him to the status of Hero.

-- We still need them --

Our heroes are **not** more crucial influences in the development of our own personality and character than our parents and siblings, or teachers, or other people that are in our daily or weekly lives. But who we choose to be our heroes, particularly during childhood and adolescence, does impact who we become. Even as adults we probably have role models that we have idolized out of their humanity.

Choosing a hero is a delicate business, one that shouldn't be undertaken frivolously. For the heroes that we choose, whether real or imagined, from the world of fact or the pages of fiction, will determine to a greater or lesser degree the things that we do and ultimately, if we allow them the privilege, the lives we will lead. (Canadian story-teller Stuart McLean's monologue, "Stamps")

We might be reluctant in our adult sophistication to call them our heroes, but there are figures we have never actually met that we emulate. Inventor-entrepreneurs create mental images -- idealized versions -- of Edison, the Wright Brothers, or Steve Jobs to inspire their own creative industry. Politicos imagine themselves modeling Jefferson, Lincoln, FDR, Kennedy, or Reagan. Old guys shooting hoops bellow, as they throw up a falling-away jumper, "Boom baby!" imagining they are Reggie Miller beating the Knicks at the buzzer. Those sorts of abstract mentors, whether called heroes or not, still have significance for our seasoned but still developing selves.

Heroes carry meanings for us, like cherished memories. They maintain a special place in our consciousness. As ideals to try to live up to, they help shape us into who we are and who we want to become. The mythologist Joseph Campbell claimed that the hero myth is culturally universal for all peoples. Carl Jung and Sigmund Freud agreed that the human mind contains an archetype of The Hero which is manifested in our myths, legends, and stories.

Whether mythological, legendary, historical, fictional, or contemporary, our heroes inhabit our minds like memories of our own achievements and failures, pushing and pulling us as we make our way through life. We bring them into consciousness when we need inspiration. They harass us when we don't want to be reminded of our shortcomings. They serve as guideposts marking the way along the paths of our lives. They can show us a better path and warn us away from a more treacherous route.

Without heroes we might be tempted into nihilism. Jack Miles, the writer, scholar, and Christian theologian, confesses in an article published in *The Sun*, "Why Religion Endures," (March 2016, p. 13) to living for ten years, while he was a young man, guided by a principle of hopeless despair. His phase of existential meaninglessness was inspired by this quote from Bertrand Russell's essay, "A Free Man's Worship":

That man is the product of causes which had no pre-vision of the end they were achieving; that his origin, his growth, his hopes and fears, his loves and his beliefs, are but the outcome of accidental collocations of atoms; that not fire, no heroism, no intensity of thought and feeling, can preserve an individual life beyond the grave; that all the labors of the ages, all the devotion, all the inspiration, all the noonday brightness of human genius, are destined to extinction in the vast death of the solar system, and that the whole temple of man's achievement must inevitably be buried beneath the debris of a universe in ruins ...

Indeed, who needs the inspiration of heroism and the brightness of human genius if we are a mere collection of atoms existing in a random universe without any higher meaning or purpose. Miles eventually found his way to a more mature and enlightened Christian faith than the strict orthodoxy of his adolescence. He was able to shed the hopelessness of living only for personal pleasure and reclaim Jesus as his hero and guiding light.

Chip Hilton and John Ritter made me want to be a better athlete and person, when I was nine. I wanted to be like Chipper and Ritter. I saw them as ideals of what boys ought to be like. They inspired me to try harder on and off the playing field. In my childish consciousness they were placed upon pedestals. From their hallowed height they could shine a light down to show me the way to become a better athlete, student, and citizen. I might have asked myself when faced with a fork in my little road, What would Chipper and Ritter do? That Ritter was a real person made him even more inspiring than the fictional Chipper. A boy growing up in Goshen, Indiana, actually could be that good!

-- But they change --

Our heroes change as we age. GI Joe is set aside for Nelson Mandela. I needed Chip Hilton and John Ritter as a kid to inspire my imagination of how I could become better than I was. They were role models that helped me to grow out of childhood. When adolescence kicked in, Chip was locked away in books I didn't read anymore.

I didn't really know John Ritter. I can't recall any conversation I ever had with him in Goshen after the pat on the back when I was nine. By the time I earned my letter sweater as a sophomore in high school, it was spring of his senior year. His classes were on the "senior floor", so it was a rare privilege to see him passing through the high school hallways between classes. I still greatly admired his athletic abilities and looked forward to seeing him lead our Redskins to victory, but my role models were changing.

Chipper and Ritter were markers in my developing psyche. After entering the "adolescent oppositional" stage, I needed to discount them as false idols or at least push them back into a corner to let them gather dust. They were not cool. They were both too straight, too goody-two shoes. Yet, they were part of me, because they had helped form me. No matter that I put away childish things, Chipper and Ritter lived on within me. As an adolescent I began to find role models in contrast to them. So, in that oppositional seeking, they were still influencing who I was becoming. And so, they still do.

A sort of surprising example I came across while writing this book was in **The Smithsonian**, "Love, Frida", by Patti Smith, January 2016. Patti Smith is no wide-eyed innocent hero-worshipper. The profile in Google describes her as "singer-songwriter, poet and visual artist who became a highly influential component of the New York City punk rock movement." Ms. Smith recounts in "Love, Frida" that her mother gave her a book on her sixteenth birthday about the artist Diego Rivera. The book included a lot of material about his lover, Frida Kahlo. Rivera and Kahlo, especially Kahlo, became Smith's role models.

I loved her. I was taken by her beauty, her suffering, her work. As a tall girl with black braids, she gave me a new way to braid my hair. Sometimes I wore a straw hat, like Diego Rivera.

Smith goes on to describe her fascination with Kahlo and how she visited Rivera and Kahlo's home in Mexico City. Smith was entranced with being able to see and touch items in the house which is now a museum. She was allowed to nap in Rivera's bed. But Smith no longer idolizes Diego and Frida the same way she did so uncritically at sixteen.

I don't mean to romanticize everything. I don't look at these two as models of behavior. Now as an adult, I understand both their great strengths and their weaknesses. Frida was never able to have children. When you have a baby you have to relinquish your self-centeredness, but they were able to act like spoiled children with each other their whole lives. Had they had children their course would have altered.

For Patti Smith, Frida and Rivera were inspiring. They pointed her in a direction when she was a teenager. As she matured, her understanding of her heroes matured. She recognized them for the flawed human beings they were. But she still recognizes and values their influence on her and on her art.

Just as our memories of personal experiences exist in our consciousness to give life meaning and to make us who we are as we collect them, so do our chosen heroes. We abstract heroes from actual and ordinary experiences of life to create a private pantheon in our minds. When we are young and immature, we need our heroes to inhabit this inner temple where we can worship them. As we become more sophisticated with age, the edifice might crack and pillars fall knocking some of the heroes tumbling into irrelevance in our lives. But, because it is a private pantheon accessible only in our own minds, even as adults or old codgers, we might pay a secret visit. Or, we might not be embarrassed at all to make public displays of our hero worship.

    At any age, heroes as mentors are life guides and sources of inspiration. If we turn cynical, they may become objects of envy. We can tear them down just as we built them up. When feeling insecure, or like a failure, we might fear that they are looking down upon us in icy judgment. Feeling like a failure, or disappointed in how life has turned out, may to some extent be a consequence of not living up to our heroes. But they are not actually judging us, we are judging ourselves in comparison to them. The disappointment is ours to own, if we fall short in our attempts to "be like Mike". Michael Jordan doesn't know that we failed to make varsity, or didn't get the job we wanted, didn't get picked by the casting director, or were unable to close the sale. So don't blame or resent him.

    Maturity should bring calculation into who we choose as heroes and how realistically we understand them. They are useful to us as guides that point the way toward our chosen goals in life and as beacons that light up the ideals we are trying to live by. But the life choices we make, which lead to our own conquests and travails, successes and failures, are our responsibilities. The direction we choose may be influenced by the heroes that move us. And we might experience pain by not living up to the ideals that our heroes exemplify. But the choice of heroes, just like the decisions we make in our life journey, is our own responsibility.

    Less evolved personalities may try to deny any truths about their heroes that do not sync up with the cherished image. A friend shared an anecdote about a friend of his who was banned from his family reunions. The Dodsons (not the real name) were tremendously proud of their ancestor who had been a drummer boy in the Civil War. The family legend, passed down through the generations, was that Ezra Dodson had dropped his drum during a battle, picked up a musket and then shot up and routed a group of charging Rebs. Cousin Rob was an amateur historian and eventually got around to researching Ezra. He discovered that Ezra had indeed dropped his drum, and then high-tailed it out of the battle. Ezra was a deserter and a coward; not a hero. Rob brought his research to the next family reunion. Instead of being thanked he was ordered to leave. The family was incensed that Rob tried to share this revised history of their great-great-grandfather. The Dodsons had no interest in re-interpreting their ancestral hero. Rob was drummed out of the family.

When considering how John Ritter was treated in his hometown by the Chamber of Commerce, we might remember the warning Jesus gave, that a prophet is not honored in his hometown. I can't help but think that, if what Dean told me is true, that the Chamber was embarrassed by what John had become. They didn't want to deal with a fallen hero. I still find it very hard to accept. Maybe a drinking problem would have disqualified John from some jobs, but, when I was growing up in Goshen, I knew of attorneys, doctors, teachers, and city officials that either had, or it was rumored they had, drinking problems. But how else can his rejection by The Chamber be explained? Like a prophet who tells his community inconvenient truths, a fallen hero might be too uncomfortable for a community to bear. Better that he leave town and not come back.

John's rejection by his hometown, his alienation from IU Nation, and his chosen isolation, reflect an inability, both by the community and John himself, to deal with a living hero that does not live up to expectations. His community rejected him, and John wanted to reject himself. He no longer wanted to be "that John Ritter".

-- Empathy for our heroes --

Psychology teaches us that repressing bad memories is a defense mechanism. We try to rid ourselves of painful memories to end the pain and avoid further trauma. But psychiatrists tell us that we must dredge up these suppressed memories to achieve mental and emotional health. We are harming ourselves further by not dealing with the pain and trauma. Healing can only come with dealing.

If Sigmund Freud had it right, then we should do the same with our heroes. We should eventually hold them up to the bright light of scrutiny and try to see them for who they really are/were. If not, they are mere idols. And we've been warned off worshipping idols since Moses received the Ten Commandments.

The Women's Movement in the 1970s protested against the objectification of women. The argument was that by treating women as sex objects, whether in film, literature, the workplace, or home, it becomes easier to victimize them. Objectification leads to victimization. Feminists were demanding to be treated as fully human. Equality with men under the law and in wages paid were not the only demands. Feminists wanted the pedestal kicked out from under them. They rejected the 1950s patriarchal-culture which protected and patronized them. They cared more about being treated as equals to men than being taken care of as "the lady of the house", "my ole lady", or "Joe's bitch", depending on your language demographic. Feminists preferred to have the glass ceiling smashed than the door opened for them by gentlemen.

The demands for equal rights by women and minorities is fundamentally a plea that all people understand each other as human beings. Real historical progress is achieved, not when women and men are interchangeable, and not when equality means sameness, but when we understand each others' similarities and differences. Equality under the law should be a given. Gender, racial, ethnic, and sexual orientation differences can be celebrated, or at least respected, rather than ridiculed or used as excuses for repression. When that occurs between individuals, and is achieved within communities, empathy is the result.

Whenever we objectify a person, or class of people, understanding is blocked. Recognizing every other person as no more and no less a human being is the beginning of compassion/empathy = feeling with. When maturity and wisdom are achieved, we need not look upon historical or living heroes as gods to be worshipped (or destroyed). They are human beings.

    Mature empathy is not just sympathetic feeling for. It includes judgment. We have the right and duty to hold our heroes to higher standards. To be a hero means to be special, to be better than normal. So, an aspect of the feeling with of compassion is an evaluation of whether a hero deserves to be looked up to as a role model.

    Investigative journalism can play a useful role in our public evaluation of a hero. It's appropriate to consider evidence of a public figure's misdeeds and hypocritical conduct in evaluating whether we want to vote for her, buy his music, or cheer for him at the next game.

    Former Speaker of the House Denny Hastert deserves all the bad publicity he has received for being a serial child molester. His reputation and life as a political leader should be destroyed. Due to the statute of limitations on the major crimes he's admitted committing, the Law cannot give him his just desserts in prison time. So, public humiliation as an element of punishment is especially appropriate in the Hastert case.

    Sometimes grocery store magazines, paparazzi, and social media mavens are too quick to leap on an ethical slip, moral failing, or embarrassment of a public figure in their efforts to attract readers/viewers with sensationalistic reports. Do we really need to demand a humiliating apology, as well as exact a fine and suspension, when a 24-year old pro athlete is overheard making a joke about race, gender, ethnicity, or any of the other protected categories of political correctness? Maybe. But the best response includes one of understanding, not just knee jerk condemnation (or praise).

    An example of a rush to harsh judgment was the piling on by the media of poor Britney Spears in 2007. She shaved her head, beat her ex-husband's SUV with an umbrella, and lost custody of her two children. These and other incidents of bizarre public behavior were splashed across the pages of tabloids but also reported in respectable media outlets. She was judged an out-of-control angry nut job. Turns out she is probably bi-polar and was not properly medicated. "A deluded 26-year-old has lost her bearings and her two small children. And we're queuing up for a peek and a snigger." ("Comment & Debate: Blame us all for Britney: As the obsessive coverage of this tear-stained wreck shows, mental illness has become a spectator sport," Peter Preston, **The Guardian**, Jan. 7, 2008, p. 28)

It's one thing to judge compassionately, it's quite another to be harshly judgmental. Empathy as compassionate judgment should be the method used in deciding who we want to place on the pedestal of hero, and who should be knocked off it.

Fictional heroes have the advantage and disadvantage of their lives being limited to pages or film. But even those heroes are not static. Critics evaluate and reevaluate the meaning of literary and cinematic figures. Great literary figures are reinterpreted with the passing of time. Macbeth, Othello, Hamlet, and the other great Shakespearean characters have been interpreted by dramatists a hundred different ways. Jane Wyatt's character as the devoted housewife/mother in *Father Knows Best* is probably perceived in an entirely different light by Millennials than the World War II generation or by Baby Boomers.

Historical and living heroes can move us and we can honor them without the need to understand them as absolutely and entirely perfect. With maturity and wisdom comes clear-sightedness and no longer a need to idolize or demonize those who were the heroes of our childhood (or later in life).

In Steven Spielberg's 2012 movie, *Lincoln*, Daniel Day-Lewis's portrayal of Honest Abe was that of a troubled, conflicted, stoic, sad, tough, clever, and sly politician, President, and person. This cinematic version of our most admired (and hated) President offers to viewers a sensitive and sophisticated understanding of how he grappled with the terrible issues he confronted during the Civil War. Admiration of Lincoln should not be lessened because we better understand his complex personality. It might not be crystal clear to what extent he really did, or did not, care about and try to move the country in a direction that was guided by the values of Truthfulness (what would now be called Transparency), Equality, and Reconciliation. How honest was Abe as a politician? It depended.

What is clear is that Lincoln was an amazing juggler. There were competing interests and factions in his Cabinet, in the Republican Party, in the Congress. The country was divided over slavery, States' rights, and by outright civil war. Lincoln had to fight his own personal demons, as well as political opponents in the North and the armies of the South. He could not afford to be strictly orthodox and loyal to any one particular value. He had to juggle many to pursue his over-arching goal of reuniting the United States of America.

If we really care to understand Lincoln as a human being, we must recognize that he may have valued the high-minded principles we like to associate with his memory, but he was not a divine embodiment of them. And so, at times, he compromised and ignored his highest principles -- because, unlike a god or mythical hero, Lincoln was human.

If we clearly see the humanity of a Washington, Lincoln, Jackie Robinson, or Neil Armstrong, we can be even more inspired by what inspired them. We can also gain insight into how to cope with competing values and influences as our heroes did in their own lives. If we can do that, we might not be too judgmental when living heroes disappoint us. Rather than idolize or demonize Mohammad Ali, Bill Clinton, Mike Tyson, Eliot Spitzer, or John Ritter, we can honor, criticize, and try to understand them. They may be heroes to some, and despised by others, but they are human beings with faults and virtues.

James McWilliams, in the previously referenced article, "The Examined Lie", urges "the curious seeker of historical truth, driven by virtue and a quest for justice," to "'enter into an empathetic relationship with people of the past: to imagine their experiences and feelings, mourn their suffering and deaths and celebrate their triumphs.'" (quoting ***The Past Within Us: Media, Memory, History***, by Tessa Morris-Suzuki)

When we take a mature view as seekers of truth, heroes need not stand apart or above us. Empathy is especially called for when heroes are still alive. We might still put them on a pedestal, but one not so high above us. It's really hard to see clearly when you're looking up at someone's feet.

Chapter Twelve

The Burden of Fame and Expectation

"I'm not John Ritter anymore."

Fame is a burden for some people. The Kardashians and Donald Trumps of the world relish all the attention they can get. My wife and I described our little boys excessive demands for candy, dessert, toys, or attention as, "too much is never enough". The excessive appetite for Me Me Me! applies to many of the reality TV stars that have managed to grab our attention. Some have not lived to regret it. The ***Hollywood Reporter*** ran a story in April 2013 entitled, "The Dark Side of Reality TV: 27 Tragic Deaths". On the other hand, some truly talented people who become well known, because they have actually made positive contributions to their communities, might feel uncomfortable with the scrutiny that comes with being in the public eye.

Famous athletes, musicians, actors, and entertainers have to live up to the expectations of their audiences for outstanding performances, if they want to maintain their popularity. Successful politicians and respected preachers known for their oratorical skills better keep their listeners enthralled or the donations to their campaign coffers and offering plates will decline. Who is going to pay the princely sum demanded by top trial lawyers, if they dud out with the jury? Winning is demanded and great performances are expected of those who aspire to reach the pinnacle in a public career.

John Ritter expressed relief to be finished with playing on the main stage of college basketball in the interview he gave after his last performance as an IU Hoosier. How long had he carried that burden? He was recognized by sports-mad boosters in Goshen as a future star before he graduated from junior high school. Sources inform me that John's father managed to arrange his work schedule to attend John's basketball and baseball practices beginning in junior high school. Papa Ritter's scrutiny at John's practices continued all the way through high school.

"Mr. Ritter was not over-bearing or out of line in any way at practice. He just sat there quietly but intently watching," John's teammate, Sam, told me. Sam described Mr. Ritter as "very likable". But, he added, "Even though Mr. Ritter was pleasant, it was different having your dad there. It would have been more pressure." Coach Mirer agreed it was strange to have a father routinely attend practice. "I'm sure it put a little extra pressure on John."

It was weird. Dads did not plan their schedules around their kids' team practices back in those days. Dads worked and moms might pick you up from practice, if you needed a ride home. But the concept of the "involved father" had not yet germinated in the American psyche during the 1960s (not in Goshen, anyway). John might have had a great relationship with his dad. But, to be the only member of the team whose father was watching him practice day after day certainly must have added a layer of pressure to perform that no other kid on the team felt.

By the time John was a senior in high school, along with his dad, Coach Lou Watson was on the bench watching John at every practice, as Coach Mirer said, "to make sure John stayed committed to Indiana basketball." John was expected to be the star of the team by his teammates, his coaches, our high school, Goshen, and then by the rabid fans at IU and eventually, The General. Through all of this John's father sat quietly watching him. No wonder he was looking forward to being relieved of the pressure by the time he finished playing for Bob Knight.

Because he didn't agree to let me interview him, I can only guess at how it felt and feels to be John Ritter. I did find clues to John's inner life before and after his star began to fade.

That his father watched John practice sports day after day, I think, is a notable piece of evidence. I'm pretty sure John loved his father and wanted to perform up to his dad's expectations. Each of John's high school teammates I've spoken with describe Mr. Ritter as a gentle and unobtrusive presence at team practices. Still, it put pressure on John no other member of the team had to deal with.

Coach Mirer's response, when I told him about my encounter with John as a 9-year old baseball player: "That's exactly how I'd expect John to act, to congratulate a younger kid. He was a role model for younger players. He was just a great kid, and a joy to coach."

If asked whether he was a sports hero, John's proper Midwestern upbringing would have required him humbly to deny being anything more than just a pretty good ball player that got some breaks.

However John Ritter thought of himself when he was a star player, when he denied himself and walked away from a high school classmate, that was a pretty clear indication that he had rejected his former public persona. John must have wanted to be free of any responsibility he owed classmates, fans, the public, for being the John Ritter we looked up to.

The John Ritter that had to be perfect had died. Another John Ritter emerged that was finally free of all the pressure the younger one had to cope with.

-- Death or Glory --

We prefer our heroes' lives to end in death or glory. We like them to be, in Bob Dylan's words, forever young. It's a bit uncomfortable for admirers to witness a hero's slow decline and decay. We don't like our heroes to be diminished by ill health and linger on past their usefulness. Heroes are not supposed to collect Social Security and drift hacking and coughing toward an inglorious death. He is still treated with reverence, but we certainly prefer the images of Muhammad Ali in his youthful rambunctious-splendor to those of the old man with Parkinson's disease. Chip Hilton will always be young, muscularly rangy, clean shaven, with a lock of blond hair listing onto his forehead as he readies himself to take a swing of the bat or shoot a free throw. Not so, John Ritter.

Martin Luther King, Jr. would not have become the venerated saint of the civil rights movement had he not died a martyr's death. Gandhi would not be Gandhi, advocate of passive resistance and father of modern India, had he not been assassinated while still the spiritual leader and mentor to the politicians who would follow him and actually govern a country. Jesus would not be Christ the Savior had he not died on the cross. Being both God and human Jesus had the advantage of the ability to come back from the dead. But all those who achieve the status of historical hero are resurrected in a way. We dredge them up from our collective memory to parade them around on commemorative occasions.

When we want to inspire the masses to action or hold up an example for our young people, heroes are called upon. It is easier to erect monuments, sculpt statues, and post commemorative plaques to the war dead than to deal with heroes who age ungracefully or come back from war or the playing field broken and damaged.

The Chicago Bears were the nearest and dearest NFL team for football fans in Northern Indiana. The 1985 Bears team that finally won a Super Bowl after years of frustrating mediocrity was a dream finally come true for long-time Bears fans. We loved the wonderful cast of characters on that team as much for their charm and joie de vive as the victories they won for us. It's been very tough as time goes by to see these men, some of them younger than me, wither and die. The greatest of them all, Walter Payton, died in 1999 of untreatable liver disease. Dave Duerson committed suicide in 2011 leaving a note that he wanted his brain to be preserved for research into chronic traumatic-encephalopathy, because he thought he had been brain-damaged by football-related concussions. William Perry, the beloved and jovial "Refrigerator", suffers from severe chronic-neuropathy and diabetes requiring constant nursing care. He's lost all his money and survives on social security. It was especially painful to see Jim McMahon, the loquacious and wild and crazy quarterback of that championship team, slurring his words, due to early onset dementia, in a televised interview about sports-related concussions. Would they give up their Super Bowl rings in exchange for their health and well-being?

Kids grow up in towns like Goshen, Indiana, dreaming of being like their heroes. Nathan Hale, hero of the American Revolution, died by hanging at the hands of the British for spying. Generations of school boys and girls have learned his inspiring last words, "I only regret that I have but one life to lose for my country." Little chests swell with pride reading about the bravery of the 21-year old lieutenant and patriotic martyr to the cause of liberty. As we mature and, one hopes, gain more wisdom, martyrdom might not seem so attractive. It might be necessary or inevitable, but the seasoning of adult experience suggests it is not personally desirable. As Jesus prayed, "Father, if possible, let this cup pass from me ..." And then on the cross, "My God, my God, why have you forsaken me?"

Meriwether Lewis, the great American explorer of the Lewis and Clark expedition, is remembered for his valiant leadership of the Corps of Discovery. His team mapped the West, found an overland-river route to the Pacific, established trade with native tribes, studied the biology of flora and fauna, and made ethnographic notes about people they encountered. The Lewis and Clark expedition is probably the US's most significant contribution to exploration, until Neil Armstrong walked on the Moon.

Lewis returned a national hero. He was granted 1,600 acres of land and appointed Governor of the Louisiana Territory by President Thomas Jefferson. These are the facts of

Lewis's life school children learn. They are less likely to be taught that he was a lousy politician and not an able administrator, became a drunken debtor, and probably committed suicide. (He might have been murdered. The circumstances of his death are still debated by historians.)

Unease developed about Meriwether Lewis as the public became aware of the unfortunate turns of his life and the troubling circumstances of his death. He began manifesting dissociative behavior in the last months of his life, talking to himself in public places and randomly changing his mind about what to do and where to go. Had he died heroically at the end of the expedition, there would be no discomfort about Lewis deserving a place in the American pantheon of national heroes.

We are more comfortable with heroes as martyrs, or those that have the decency to die young, than to see them fail physically, mentally, or emotionally. Heroes are not supposed to have the same flaws as our friends and neighbors, or us.

-- Duel-edged sword of fame and glory --

In Book 11 of Homer's **Odyssey**, Odysseus visits Achilles in the underworld. During his lifetime, Achilles was the greatest warrior of all the Greeks in the Trojan War. It had been foretold that he would die a hero's death by joining his fellow Greeks in the war. But the prophecy also offered an alternative fate. Achilles could avoid the draft (so to speak) and live a long life but would not become the greatest hero of his age. The young warrior chose to fulfill his destiny and was killed in battle before Troy was conquered.

Odysseus is curious to find out from Achilles what it's like to be the greatest of all the slain heroes in Hades. He assumes it must be a pretty good gig, so he addresses Achilles as, "blessed in life, blessed in death". To Odysseus's surprise, Achilles retorts that he would rather be a slave to the worst of masters than be king of all the dead. In Hades, Achilles wishes he would have forsaken his destiny to become the greatest hero of the Greeks. He'd like a do-over.

I wonder, would John Ritter have preferred never to have been *The* John Ritter after he had become a shade of his former self, when he was alone and homeless? Had he never been famous and the idol of Hoosier basketball fans his life might have taken a more ordinary course. John was a brilliant student, so he might have landed a well-paying job in industry or the professions with domestic tranquility to follow and eventually dandling grandchildren on his knee. I don't know exactly how John feels about the way his life has gone. But it was pretty clear he knew what his destiny should be and he worked hard to achieve it. John Ritter wasn't just talented, he was known for his work ethic and hustle. He labored to fulfill the destiny Goshen boosters expected of him; to become that John Ritter, our local hero.

Odysseus tries to impress Achilles by telling him of the great honors with which the other Greek warriors have treated Achilles' corpse. Achilles is unimpressed. It no longer matters to him, now that he is dead, to be worshipped as the Greeks' greatest warrior. But then, ambiguity enters the conversation. He wants to know how his son Neoptolemus is doing. Odysseus tells Achilles that Neoptolemus too has gained the status of hero due to his bravery and conquests in the Trojan war. Achilles beams (to the extent shades can beam) with pride in his son. Despite the wisdom gained from his own experience, that there is a definite downside to heroism -- you're likely to have to pay the ultimate price, because people come after you -- Achilles still takes pride in his son being idolized as a hero.

What did Achilles actually want for his son?

Fame is required to transform noble action into heroism. Someone who performs wonderful deeds may be worthy of the status of hero, but if we know not who she is, she will not be remembered as a hero.

People may become famous and not be heroic. That has

become absurdly true with modern mass media and the pop-cultural expectation that everyone deserves fifteen minutes of fame. Paris Hilton and the Kardashians are internationally known, but, as far as I know, are not heroic. They are scrutinized because of their fame as celebrities, but they do not live under the burden of expectation that they will perform heroically or live exemplary lives.

Counter-intuitively in the current age in which fame is so desirable, it is fame that makes the mantle of hero so heavy to wear. Being a famous hero creates expectation -- you have to live up to it. If Michael Jordan scored lots of points in regular-season games, but always missed the shot needed to win critical games at the buzzer, he would have been demoted from "the greatest" to a very good basketball player. Jordan had to deal with the pressure and live up to the expectations of his fans to come through in the crucial moments of the big games. Otherwise, his stock as a sports hero would fall.

Being famous creates scrutiny -- the public is fascinated by famous people. We relish our cult of celebrity where validation is conferred by coverage in **People Magazine**, an interview on the TV show *Extra*, clicks and likes in social media. But we expect more from our heroes. They are not just celebrities. We require more from them than titillation or entertainment. Because we identify with them. We need them and they owe us.

But to become a hero to the community, nation, or world, the hero must become famous. She must become widely known and enter her culture's consciousness. The public develops stories about the hero which are circulated. The stories are remembered and tales of the hero's great deeds are passed on to the next generation. (My favorite football player of all time was Walter Payton. My sons never saw Payton play live, but they had a poster of him in their bedroom.) The actual person who has become a famous hero, whether for winning games for the home team, saving comrades in battle, or leading a human rights movement, cannot escape. She is trapped by fame in that identity, which brings scrutiny and expectation.

Whether it is through the retelling of ancient legends, historical records, our current mass communications and social media, fame is gained by eye and ear, and then spread by mouth in the telling (or by YouTube posts). It can travel across villages, cities, states, countries, or continents, or stop at the town borders. Few of those who strive for excellence in sport, art, politics, war, or business do not desire it. Like Achilles, no matter what the cost to our lives, fame is as attractive as treasure. Many of us want it. If the stars align so that with talent, drive, hard work, and lucky breaks, you are rewarded with fame, from the underworld, Achilles might advise you to run and hide. But you probably won't.

Many of us crave our fifteen minutes. Whether it comes from years of hard work in the gym, laboratory, art studio, at the keyboard, or the rubber chicken circuit of political gatherings, those who have the drive strive for it.

The desire for attention spurs us to post cat videos and cutesy images of babies in social media. The desire for attention in order to achieve infamy is one of the motives for massacring children in a school, students on a college campus, or fellow employees. Of course the relative consequences as between being subjected to amateur dance performance videos on Facebook and mass murders are dramatically different. But still, underlying all these efforts to gain attention is it not the urge for a moment of fame or infamy? Don't we hope that what we post will "go viral"? Aren't terrorists hoping for the same?

The ability to achieve instant, if short-lived, fame on YouTube and social media has created a mad scramble for it. It is like the California Gold Rush of 1848. We drive ourselves over metaphorical hills and across valleys to get more followers, "friends", clicks, and views.

In *Henry V* Shakespeare put into words and out of the mouth of the young warrior-king the glory to be won by his soldiers in the wonderful speech before the battle with the French on St. Crispian's day:

> *If we are mark'd to die, we are enow*
> *To do our country loss; and if to live,*
> *The fewer men, the greater share of honour.*
> *God's will! I pray thee, wish not one man more.*
> *By Jove, I am not covetous for gold,*
> *Nor care I who doth feed upon my cost;*
> *It yearns me not if men my garments wear;*
> *Such outward things dwell not in my desires:*
> *But if it be a sin to covet honour,*
> *I am the most offending soul alive. ...*
> *Rather proclaim it, Westmoreland, through my host,*
> *That he which hath no stomach to this fight,*
> *Let him depart; his passport shall be made*
> *And crowns for convoy put into his purse.*
> *We would not die in that man's company*
> *That fears his fellowship to die with us.*
> *This day is called the feast of Crispian.*
> *He that outlives this day, and comes safe home,*
> *Will stand a tip-toe when the day is named,*
> *And rouse him at the name of Crispian.*
> *He that shall live this day, and see old age,*
> *Will yearly on the vigil feast his neighbours,*
> *And say "To-morrow is Saint Crispian."*
> *Then will he strip his sleeve and show his scars.*
> *And say "These wounds I had on Crispin's day."*
> *Old men forget; yet all shall be forgot,*
> *But he'll remember with advantages*
> *What feats he did that day, then shall our names*
> *... Be in their flowing cups freshly remember'd.*
> *This story shall the good man teach his son;*
> *And Crispin Crispian shall ne'er go by,*
> *From this day to the ending of the world,*
> *But we in it shall be remember'd;*
> *We few, we happy few, we band of brothers;*

For he to-day that sheds his blood with me
Shall be my brother; be he ne'er so vile,
This day shall gentle his condition,
And gentlemen in England now a-bed
Shall think themselves accursed they were not here,
And hold their manhoods cheap whiles any speaks
That fought with us upon Saint Crispin's day.

To fight for Honor, Glory, and Fame, what more could a soldier want? Whether you're scarred for life or die, you'll be remembered!

Yeah, right.

In the gold rush to glory, a cost/benefit analysis of fame is rarely contemplated. We are like the miser who drowns trying to swim across the river weighed down with his treasure.

If it is only fifteen minutes, fame could just be a kick-up-your-heels fun experience. You can hang the picture on your wall and tell your kids about it. But what if the craving continues unsatisfied? You probably know someone who was briefly in the spotlight, or someone who never even got their fifteen minutes, and has lived with disappointment ever since. Fame is a flame that can burn you whether you touch it or not.

For a couple years I taught a class titled, "Changing Directions in Life", for the older-adult organization Oasis. During a class discussion, one of the students stated that she was 70-years old and her life ambition was to become a famous artist. "Nora" took the class, she said, because she was about to give up on her goal but hoped she would learn from the class how she could yet achieve her ambition. Nora had been doing art her entire adult life, but hadn't become famous. She was quite disappointed when I reminded her that the purpose of the class was to help students better understand how to handle major changes in their lives. The course was not a road map to fame for an ageing yet still aspiring artist. I tried to explain that, from an existential point of view, being an artist was living an authentic life. She had the power and freedom to choose to live that life or not. Seeking fame was not existentially authentic, because it was the world, not Nora, that would bestow or not bestow fame upon her. She would have none of it and left the class disappointed.

    Before joining the gold rush for fame, it might be wise to consider whether it really is worth it. Do the benefits merit the costs. Homer's Achilles stands beyond the gates of Hades warning those who think it is worth it to die young and leave a beautiful corpse to think it through. Football players suffering dementia by the time they are fifty years old might wish they could have a re-do and try a different sport.

    I don't know whether John Ritter considers his years as a star athlete worth the price he paid for it. I don't know to what extent, if any, he blames the burden of being John Ritter, the star player who did not make it in the NBA, on his spiral downward into divorce, depression, and drinking. But I think he would have understood the warning of Achilles. When he had heard enough from Odysseus about his son, Achilles turned his broad back and walked away from Odysseus. John asked nothing of his old friend Dean from Goshen. He simply turned his broad back and walked away after denying he was John Ritter anymore.

    If a hero can no longer be heroic and her life becomes a quotidian snore, god bless her. Rather than being uncomfortable with an Ali suffering from Parkinson's or a Bronze Star winner returning from Afghanistan a paraplegic, are we capable of honoring them for their great deeds and feel with them in their suffering? They gave much for us. So, when they can no longer carry the burden of expectation and no longer perform extraordinary deeds, let's give them a break. It's only in comic books and bad epic poetry that heroes are invulnerable. Only in an untimely death do real-live heroes remain forever young.

    John Ritter became a homeless cab driver. He turned

his back on making a living in the world of athletics, to which he had given most of his life and from which he had received many rewards but not the highest -- a pro contract. A decade later he left behind the life of corporate executive, husband, and father. Was that because he just couldn't deal with the pressures of a "regular" job and family responsibilities? Had he grown so tired of carrying the burden of fulfilling the expectations of others and his own, that he let it drop and ran away?

If he had a posse or community that had his back, there would have been comradeship and support to help ease him into a life after basketball or at least cushion his fall when he became depressed and struggled with the demon alcohol. Had the Goshen Chamber of Commerce responded with courage and compassion instead of rejection, that might have halted his downward spiral. He could have built a new life coaching basketball in the Goshen area, like his younger brother Mike. Or, like many other high school sports stars, John could have capitalized on his name recognition and sold insurance, real estate, or cars. Why not? Those were all possibilities for the former star of the hometown Redskins.

In high school and college John Ritter was too "good" to fit comfortably into the normal society of classmates and teammates. His orthodoxy to 1950s values and standards of conduct were higher than his fellows. He stood out as a shining example of what the grown-ups wanted kids to be like. When he was a middle-aged drunk in need of a job, he was not good enough for "the grown-ups" in Goshen to lend a helping hand.

Is this a paradox or irony? John lived up to such high standards when he was young he made other kids feel slightly uncomfortable in the sense that they couldn't feel close to him. Later, he made the Chamber of Commerce feel uncomfortable, because he wasn't living up to their standards. The further irony or paradox is that John might have been that rare star athlete that didn't actually care about the fame his heroics generated. High school friends describe him as so shy and humble he could fade into the background of social groups, even though he was the brightest star in the school.

John's exceptional talent as an athlete and his extraordinary personal virtue set him apart, and made him locally famous whether he wanted it or not. Instead of eliciting compassion in a time of need, John's fame created a problem for the powers that be in the local community. They didn't know how to deal with him, so they sent him away.

Fame is a fire that attracts. Without a firm grounding in a caring community, it is likely to burn. When the hero can no longer meet our needs, the community ought to try to meet his rather than turn him out.

To become the most famous boxer of all time, Muhammad Ali had to take the many blows to his head that has left him crippled. Would he undo that if he could? Whether he would or not, he has a loving wife and family, and he is still heralded by adoring fans whenever he appears in public. That he has been loved and cared for by family and friends has surely helped cushion the blows Muhammad Ali still feels.

Like Achilles and Ali, John Ritter chose his fate. He gave his blood, sweat, and tears to become the star of the Goshen Redskins and IU Hoosiers. So, why did he let go of the life and rewards his hard work had earned him? And, why was the community not there for him in his time of need?

Dealing with fame and the expectations it brings is a challenge the hero must face. Dealing with the inability to perform heroically and live up to the expectations of self and others may be an even greater challenge for an ageing hero. Losing his marriage, job, and athletic physique, no longer praised by those in charge of the established order, John Ritter would face a foe even more daunting than Bill Walton and the UCLA Bruins. He had to meet this challenge alone, and the foe was himself.

Chapter Thirteen

Heroes, History, and Symbols

Anybody here seen my old friend Abraham?
Can you tell me where he's gone?
He freed lotta people but it seems the good they die young
You know I just looked around and he's gone

Anybody here seen my old friend John?
Can you tell me where he's gone?
He freed lotta people but it seems the good they die young
I just looked around and he's gone

Anybody here seen my old friend Martin?
Can you tell me where he's gone?
He freed lotta people but it seems the good they die young
I just looked around and he's gone

Didn't you love the things that they stood for?
Didn't they try to find some good for you and me?
And we'll be free
Some day soon, it's gonna be one day

Anybody here seen my old friend Bobby?
Can you tell me where he's gone?
I thought I saw him walkin' up over the hill
With Abraham, Martin, and John

"Abraham, Martin And John," lyrics by Dion

Heroes, symbols, and historical memory converge when the community or nation is called upon to act as one. National flags and team mascots, collective memories of great victories, and beloved figures from the past are invoked to unify the nation to support going to war or just to cheer on the home team.

> *Wave the flag of old Chicago,*
> *Maroon the color grand.*
> *Ever shall her team be victors*
> *Known throughout the land.*
> *With the grand old man to lead them,*
> *Without a peer they'll stand.*
> *Wave again the dear old banner,*
> *For they're heroes ev'ry man.*

Fight song of my alma mater, University of Chicago

Soldiers bellow the names of revered figures (For Stonewall!) or battle cries based on a collective memory (Remember the Maine!) while waving flags with the national symbol as they charge the enemy. Players, cheerleaders, and fans wave pennants of the team's colors while shouting cheers for their champions. Political parties hoist banners of their historical standard bearers to claim their legacies at party conventions. Republicans hoot and bellow when Ronald Reagan's name is invoked at a party rally. Democrats roar approval when a speaker references FDR or JFK.

A hero's identity becomes associated with a particular historical event and the hero becomes a symbol of the significance of that event to the community or nation. The hero's name is cited to give credibility to a cause, to drum up support, as a call for resolute action. Abraham, Martin, and John were human beings but merged into symbols of the peace and civil rights movements, as Dion's song poignantly reminds us.

The hero is transformed from a human being into a source to be cited. If you can convince Republicans that Ronnie would have supported this candidate or that bill, then by god we should too! If Democrats believe this initiative is part of the Roosevelt-Kennedy-Johnson progressive legacy, then we surely ought to line up behind it. These political heroes have become historical precedents to be followed.

Our heroes are treated the way trial courts treat the historical decisions of the appellate courts -- not just with respect, but they must be followed. If lower courts do not follow the precedents of higher courts, the judicial system is not functioning the way it is supposed to and it breaks down. When the people do not follow and emulate their heroes, then the foundations of the community are threatened. We will lose our way as a society, if we forget our heroes and what they stand for.

-- Mutability of the meaning of Hero --

What if we leap out of the trenches to follow the battle cry of the hero but the battle is lost? History is written by the victors. Heroes who let us down will be tarnished, and, if they let us down too often, they will be evicted from the pantheon. Same with a culture's or nation's collective memory of a significant historical event. It can be reinterpreted or thrown into the dustbin of irrelevance.

History does not just happen and is then permanently fixed forever. Its meaning can be changed or purposefully forgotten. American soldiers were less likely to shout, "Remember the Maine and to hell with Spain!" after historians cast doubt on Spanish culpability for sinking the American ship. Bill Buckner was an all-star baseball player, batting champion, and set a record for assists as a first baseman. He was a lock to be voted into the Baseball Hall of Fame, until a legacy-changing game in the 1986 World Series. What he's now remembered for by most sports fans is the flub between his legs. His name became synonymous with "screw up". Ha! You just pulled a Buckner! He is blamed (unfairly) for the loss of the Series by the Boston Red Sox. That one error transformed him from a hero into a symbol of ineptitude in sports history.

When a culture is in transition, like our nation was during the late 1960s, history and heroes are reinterpreted. The opening up of the dominant culture to the previously powerless and disenfranchised allowed Americans to care about and learn about the heroes of black history, women's history, queer history, the labor movement, and other alternative histories to those approved by the dominant WASP culture.

In recent years American culture has retrenched and returned to more traditional values in some ways and in other ways it has incorporated the counter-culture of the 1960s into the mainstream. Most everyone in the US now accepts in principle the equality of women, minorities, and gays. Most everyone wears blue jeans and has at least tried smoking pot (even if they didn't inhale, ala Bill Clinton). The notion of what it means to be a hero (or, at least how the word is used) has expanded exponentially in our post-modern culture. Victims are as likely to be called heroes as rescuers. By the way they are described in the news media, all those who died on 9/11 are heroes. (The villainous murderers who crashed the planes are, of course, not heroes in the West. But they are to the jihadist sympathizers, who are writing history for Islamic extremists.) All military veterans, even if they never saw combat, are called heroes on network news shows, as are cops and firefighters.

This liberal reinterpretation of the term in the mass media has superficially diminished its status. This development is a dilution of the distinctive meaning of *hero* and the status of heroes. If someone time-traveled from the 19th Century and was watching television news, she might think anyone can be a hero. It's as if the effort to give everyone fifteen minutes of fame has coalesced into calling everyone a hero. Christopher Vogler asserts in **The Hero's Journey Outline** ("TheWritersJourney" blog) that, "Everyone is the hero of his or her own myth." The advent of social media has granted us the means to foist our own mythology off on the rest of the online world as heroic (or at least worthy of a moment of attention within the twitter-verse).

-- Immutability of the meaning of Hero --

But the kids don't buy it, and neither do serious people. My two boys loved their super heroes, whether in video games, comic books, TV shows, or movies. The little guys were in awe of the powers of the fictional heroes of DC and Marvel Comics and the Power Rangers. Their favorite characters could run faster, jump higher, and capture or kill bad guys. My boys' childhood heroes were not fundamentally different than my own. Batman as the Dark Knight has become a more complicated character. He is now often misunderstood, even victimized by unjust authorities and the media, but he is not just a victim. As the Dark Knight, Batman might have more psychological depth but he still kicks bad-guys' asses.

Real heroes are not just universalized firemen, cops, or soldiers. They are not ciphers to which our attention is drawn for a thirty-second bit on the local news channel. I am not denigrating the critical work that firefighters, police officers, and our soldiers do. We'd be in a terrible fix without them. Many are local heroes, and some, like Sergeant York and Chesty Puller, are national-historic heroes.

A hero to me or for you means that we have been affected in an extraordinary way by the hero. He has to mean something to us much more than just a moment of our time during a news program. We internalize our heroes and carry them with us. The mere mention of a hero's name evokes pride and passion and significance. We identify with our heroes in a special way, because they mean more to us than just an ordinary memory of someone who happened to cross our path. Heroes symbolize meanings. They are associated with significant events in our lives and to our community or nation.

The fireman that risked his life to save your life, or even your pet cat's, is a hero to you. The cop who took a bullet, but neutralized a maniac that had already shot three people in a crowded downtown mall, is a hero to the community. The Medal of Honor winner, who rescued local villagers and wounded comrades by single-handedly driving off a Taliban force that had surrounded a village, is a national hero. Regardless of the personal journeys of these rescuers, they merit being called heroes because they risked everything for you, the community, or the cause to which the nation was committed.

Hero is not limited to rescuers and to those that have risked their lives to save others. It applies to all those who have done something so extraordinary which had such a positive effect in your life, on the community, or nation, that the person and the deed are unforgettable and are forever associated with virtues such as Courage, Wisdom, or Compassion.

As adults, we might not talk about heroes per se, because with maturity we are expected to put away childish things. We probably don't gush with praise of heroes the way kids do, but we still recognize and honor the super-achievers in sports, the arts, governance, law, medicine, business, etc. Every year **Time Magazine** and a plethora of other publications come out with their Man/Woman/Person of the Year and the ten, fifty, or one hundred most important people who deserve to be recognized for excellence and superiority over the rest of us common folk. Whether we call Magic Johnson, Steve Jobs, Warren Buffet, or Stephen Hawking, genius, special, great, or hero, people who have become famous because of the superior abilities they have used to benefit others achieve a status in our culture equivalent to the traditional way the term *hero* has been used.

No matter what we call them, there are still giants

among us, who are feted in the ways cultures traditionally recognize their heroes. They are rewarded with honors, memorials, money, and attention. They deserve the honor, if, indeed, they have given us something so unforgettably beneficial that mention of their names reminds us of their extraordinary deeds. And, they have come to represent in the collective consciousness values we care about, like Ingenuity, Industriousness, or Indomitability.

-- Value of the brand --

Another cultural shift in the way heroes are treated is the opportunity for Commercialization.

The ancient Greeks were wise in many ways and their culture was as mature (and decadent) as ours in some ways. They awarded winners of the Pan-Hellenic Games (the Olympics were just one of four games) a simple wreath. The modern Olympics paid homage to this tradition by creating a hallowed cult of athletic amateurism. Avery Brundage ruled as high priest of the International Olympic Committee as its chairman from 1952 to 1972 (he was chairman of the American Olympic Committee for twenty years before assuming chairmanship of the international body). He ruled with an iron fist. Brundage banned any athlete from Olympic competition tainted as a professional by material reward from sport.

The Greeks would have found Brundage's puritanical definition bizarre. Victorious Olympians in the ancient games were showered with rewards in their home towns. The simple wreath was representative of the formal honor, but it was not all that the winners received.

For decades the IOC tried to prevent Olympic athletes from prospering materially from their athletic gifts. One of the most infuriating cases was what the governing body did to Jim Thorpe, the great American all-around athlete of Sac and Fox heritage. The IOC stripped Thorpe of the two gold medals he won in the 1912 Olympics for his victories in the decathlon and pentathlon. It was discovered that Thorpe had played minor league baseball for a couple seasons.

Think about it! Jim Thorpe accomplished what might be the greatest athletic achievement ever by winning the pentathlon and decathlon -- that's a total of fifteen events. He wore a pair of mis-matched shoes he found in a trash bin for most of the decathlon events. His own shoes were stolen after the first day of the three day decathlon competition.

The winner of the decathlon is, by tradition, called "the World's greatest athlete". The tradition began when King Gustav V of Sweden congratulated Thorpe, after he won the decathlon at the 1912 Stockholm Olympics, by saying, "You, sir, are the world's greatest athlete." Thorpe's laconic reply was simply, "Thanks." (***Smithsonian Magazine***, "Why Are Jim Thorpe's Olympic Records Still Not Recognized?", July 2015, Sally Jenkins)

The purists on the IOC expunged from Olympic records the victories of this amazing athlete. Thorpe died in poverty at the age of 66. The IOC eventually sent replica gold medals to his family in 1983, thirty years after his death. It has never restored Jim Thorpe's record-winning times and points to its official records. The second place finishers are still in the record book as the winners of the 1912 pentathlon and decathlon.

A controversy which infuriated fans and inflamed international tensions during the 1960s and 70s was whether Eastern Bloc athletes were really professionals and should, therefore, be banned from the Olympic Games. Soviet states supported their athletes with state-provided food, housing, and living stipends. Critics in the West ("free Europe" and the US) argued that competitors from the USSR and its satellites should be considered professionals, because of the subsidies their governments provided.

The IOC gave in to the geopolitical pressure from the Commies. Brundage's scales tipped in favor of "the Games must go on" for commercial reasons. The IOC feared the commercial value of the Olympics would decline, if the Soviet states withdrew. By the 1950s the IOC was raking in millions from its television and radio broadcast contracts.

After Brundage stepped down and the public got wind of its skyrocketing revenue, the IOC's own image was tarnished by exposure of its hypocrisy. The dam broke. Olympic athletes are now expected to be professionals to some extent. The way modern Olympic heroes are treated is now more consistent with the ancient Greek traditions. Winning a gold medal can be worth far more than its weight in gold.

Our consumer culture has become increasingly more aware and accepting of the commercial value of the status of hero. Not just for Olympic champions.

Commercialization of athlete-heroes reached a zenith with Michael Jordan in the 1990s. Gatorade's marketing department developed the phrase, "Be like Mike". It was everywhere Madison Avenue could reach, and sports-loving kids soon picked it up and wanted to be like Mike. Jordan became the most popular and famous sports hero, at least in the US, since Ali.

But, despite his god-like performances on the court, and seemingly stoic personality off court, Michael Jordan sort of cracked. He dropped out of basketball to fail at baseball, his reputation was stained with tales of gambling debts, and he became embroiled in a messy and very expensive divorce. It took awhile, but with hard work and dedication to his brand, his reputation has recovered. He is still in basketball management/ownership with the Charlotte Hornets and selling underwear for Hanes.

Perhaps as a defense against any possibility of incurring the burden of hero worship, Jordan's ex-teammate and cultural-freak, Dennis Rodman, assumed the public persona of anti-hero and court jester. With massive piercings and tattoos already snaking around his extremities, Rodman began wearing white wedding dresses and declared that he "wasn't nobody's role model". The nut-case ruler of North Korea, Kim Jong-un, has become his bosom buddy. Rodman wanted fame (or notoriety), but not the burden of Hero.

Most of us would probably rather be like Mike than Dennis Rodman. But I can't help but wonder which of the two are actually enjoying life more? Mike seems to want to go down in history as one of sports' greatest, while Dennis just wants some attention and to have a good time (at least that's how it looks from the outside). Rodman will probably be a blip on the historical/cultural radar, but Jordan has achieved the status of a sports icon for the ages, like Jim Thorpe, Joe Lewis, Jesse Owens, Babe Ruth, Jackie Robinson, Walter Payton, and Wayne Gretzky.

Michael Jordan will be remembered as a symbol of excellence and victory. He is a brand. And that is worth a hell of a lot of money now and for the heirs of his estate. (It was marketing genius by Nike to call what became the most popular athletic shoe, since the Converse All-Star, "Air Jordan". The founders of Nike demonstrated their business acumen from the beginning by their choice of the company's name. In the ancient Greek pagan religion, Nike was a goddess representing Victory.)

-- When culture changes, history, symbols, and heroes change --

Symbols, history, and heroes are reinterpreted as culture changes, whether through success or failure, victory or defeat. A historical movement that has recently reached a tipping point is associated with the Confederate Battle Flag. On June 17, 2015, during a prayer service, nine people were shot dead by Dylann Roof at the Emanuel African Methodist Episcopal Church in Charleston, South Carolina. The mass murder was inspired by a racist ideology associated in Roof's sick mind with his Confederate heritage. Outrage of the African-American community and its white sympathizers pressured Governor Nikki Haley to demand that the South Carolina Legislature vote to remove the Confederate Flag from the Statehouse flagpole. It came down for the last time (unless the Legislature reverses itself in the future) on July 10, 2015.

A few months later in October 2015 the University of Mississippi (Ole Miss) lowered the State Flag (presumably permanently) from its hallowed place in the center of campus. The Mississippi Flag includes the Confederate symbol. Students and the NAACP had been pressuring the university to cease flying the flag on campus. The Student Senate had passed a resolution to remove the flag. The Administration finally buckled. The Mississippi Governor and Legislature, however, have refused to consider removing the Confederate symbol from the State Flag.

In South Carolina and at Ole Miss the flags were not destroyed but consigned to historical archives. I think that is wise. History is not being denied. The Confederate Flag will be remembered, but understood more fully and sensitively. It is being reinterpreted as different points of view are incorporated into the mainstream of cultural conversation in the South.

In August 2015 the Memphis, Tennessee, City Council voted to remove a statue of Nathan Bedford Forest which has been prominently located in a city park. Forest was a Confederate general, slave trader, and first Grand Wizard of the Ku Klux Klan. To some, he is still a hero of the Confederacy. To others, he's a mass murderer and monster. What he means to the community of Memphis, the State of Tennessee, and the USA is being revised. From **Mother Jones**, "It's Time to Separate the South From the Confederacy", by Becca Andrews, Aug. 22, 2015:

At the ceremony unveiling the statue in May, 1905, nothing was said of Forrest's order to massacre more than 300 African-

American Union soldiers who had already surrendered at Fort Pillow, Tennessee, in 1864. His role as a leader in the KKK was never mentioned. Instead, the Forrest Monument Association spoke of his chivalry, and of heritage and honor.

    A more emotional, bordering on violent, removal of a statue was that of Cecil Rhodes from the University of Cape Town in South Africa in April 2015. The bronze statue was splashed with paint, slapped, whipped, and had trash thrown at it as a crane pulled the statue off its base. Some white students protested the removal. Like protesters against Confederate Flag removals in the US South, some white South Africans interpret removal of the Rhodes statue as a desecration of their heritage and an effort to delegitimize their racial/ethnic history. To many black South Africans Cecil Rhodes is a symbol of the historical humiliation of colonization and illegitimate white power.

    According to the **Mother Jones** article, black students were shouting "Amandla!" (power!) as the statue was removed. What a clear case of how heroes, symbols, and historical memory merge. They have power. When power shifts within a community or nation, so will the understanding of its heroes and symbols. History is not static. It is changed by how it is understood. Understanding is changed by the moving forces of cultural influences. The victors, those in power, not only write and interpret the history, they decide who are the heroes.

    My interpretation of the Chip Hilton and John Ritter hero stories changed with the times and my own ageing. At nine, I thought they were the perfect ideals of boyhood. As a rebellious adolescent, I thought they were uncool. Over time, they were associated with a nostalgic longing for a simpler time and way of life. In the messy confusion of urban life and moral relativism, as a father, I wanted to tell my own boys about a boy who was always true to his family and friends and lived according to the 1950s virtues of honesty, respect for authority, patriotism, and just being a good guy. Chipper was still there to be the hero of that story. But John Ritter's life journey had changed his story into a much more complicated one to tell.

John Ritter did not want to tell me his story, but I have the power (Amandla!) to create my own story of John Ritter. The final chapters of my story of John Ritter's Hero Journey follow in Part Four.

Part Four
Acceptance

The modern hero ... who dares to heed the call ... cannot, indeed must not, wait for his community to cast off its slough of pride, fear, rationalized avarice, and sanctified misunderstanding. ... It is not society that is to guide and save the creative hero, but precisely the reverse. And so every one of us shares the supreme ordeal -- carries the cross of the redeemer -- not in the bright moments of his tribe's great victories, but in the silences of his personal despair.
The Hero with a Thousand Faces, Joseph Campbell, MJF Books, 1949

The rest of the story of John Ritter's journey from Local Hero through the Abyss of Self Destruction, Redemption, and Homecoming appear in the chapters of this final Part Four. The best is saved for last.

Chapter Fourteen

Why John Ritter Ceased to Be John Ritter

I began this writing project, in part, to solve a mystery that had bothered me for years. What happened to my childhood hero and why did his life not follow the path his hometown fans expected? If John was not going to star in the NBA or ABA, like his teammate George McGinnis, why didn't John Ritter's life parallel his co-captain Steve Downing's? Without John's cooperation it would be difficult to solve the mystery.

I searched the Internet for any articles of public information I could find about John Ritter after deciding to embark on this writing project without John's cooperation. My search revealed a number of developments in John's life after his graduation from Indiana University in 1973. This chapter sets out several of the significant events that are discoverable in the free public record.

John did land a job with Eli Lilly Co. after graduating from IU, but a year later he was hired as the player-coach of the Anderson, Indiana, franchise of a new semi-pro basketball league.

*PAGE 12 **ANDERSON DAILY BULLETIN** SATURDAY, MAY 4, 1974: ALACS select experienced John Ritter as player-coach*

By DON CRONIN Bulletin Sports Editor:

Anderson's entry in the new International Basketball Association will have a player-coach, **The Bulletin** *has learned. John Ritter, former Indiana University standout, will be named player-coach of the Anderson ALACS at a news conference scheduled for today at the Holiday Inn. ALAC general manager Joe Cook called the press conference in conjunction with the IBA-league meeting today.*

League commissioner Richard L. Duncan of Dayton, Ohio, will be present for the press conference along with Phil Overman, general manager of the Ft. Wayne entry in the IBA.

Anderson joins Lafayette and Dayton and Hamilton, Ohio, in forming the South Division of the IBA. The North Division is made up of Elkhart County, Ft. Wayne, Hammond and South Bend.

Ritter, currently employed at Eli Lilly Co. in Indianapolis, confirmed that he is signing a contract to be the ALACS player-coach. "At first I was skeptical about the league," said Ritter, "because I had heard about it last summer and knew of some players who had been contacted, and in some cases signed contracts. But now, I'm impressed with the league to the point that I want to be associated with it . . . and with Joe Cook. Joe has impressed me with his attitude. He goes slow with all the preparations and tries to make sure everything is done right. He has really put in a lot of time and effort on this."

According to Cook, he will be in charge of the mechanical aspects of the ALACS. "There won't be an assistant coach," said Cook. "It's John's show. He wants to put a team on the floor which will be enjoyable to watch. I'm not from a basketball background so I'll tend to the business aspects of the franchise and let John handle what happens on the court."

Ritter feels he can call on a variety of experiences. "I was fortunate to play for one coach in high school and two others (Knight and Lou Watson) in college," he said. "So I feel like I can combine what I feel are the best parts of three ways at looking at the game. Our club will probably look somewhat like the styles of all of the people I've played for."

Ritter, who holds the IU career free throw percentage record at 86.2 per cent, helped lead the Hoosiers to the finals of the NCAA tournament as a senior. He hit free throws at a 90.8 per cent clip as a junior when he made 32 straight. The Goshen native, who was named to the 1969 Indiana High School All-Star team, has some definite ideas on what should take place with the ALACS.

"We're looking for players who are willing to work and hustle and play an exciting brand of basketball. I know people in Anderson can see a lot of good high school basketball. So, to get those people to come watch us play, we have to give them a good product. I'm taking things rather slow and looking for that type of player. We aren't the caliber of the NBA or ABA, but we'll give the people a good show with good, sound basketball. There's no doubt we can get good players for what we can pay ($70-per-game top by league rules)," said Ritter. "There are a lot of guys playing a lot of basketball on the weekends for nothing who would jump at the chance. We just have to weed them out and make sure we get top-notch people. We want players the people can look up to and won't be ashamed to bring their kids to see play basketball."

Ritter indicated he plans to hold a one or two-day tryout camp, probably in late September or early October and invite all comers!

After signing ten players to the team in the October tryouts, Coach Ritter expressed optimism about his team's chances in a subsequent ***Anderson Bulletin*** article. He wasn't able to recruit a dominant big man, so his plan was to play with "speed and hustle". "'Running will definitely be one of our strong points this year,' noted the soft-spoken Ritter."

The International Basketball Association folded after one season. The few articles I could find about the Anderson ALAC team in local papers do not mention John actually playing. So, although he was contracted as a player-coach, it seems that he coached but did not play. The Cleveland Cavaliers held the rights to him until September 1976, so it's possible they did not want him to play, but I doubt that was the reason. Perhaps John had lost his confidence as a player or begun to let go of the personal discipline needed to remain in peak physical condition. Or, maybe he just wanted to try his hand at coaching without the distraction of playing. Information about the ALAC team is quite spotty, so it may be that John played in some games, but I was unable to find reports about those games.

The team's record was worse than mediocre, 11 wins and 14 losses. They finished more than ten games behind the first place Grand Rapids Tackers, according to ***Association for***

Professional Basketball Research, APBR.org. Quotes in local newspapers from John about the team's performance expressed frustration, especially about his players' lack of commitment to playing tough defense and unselfish offense. John comes across sounding like Coach Norman Dale, the Gene Hackman coach-character in *Hoosiers*, or Bobby Knight without the anger-management issues. His style of coaching was that of a tough, demanding disciplinarian expecting every member of his team to give their maximum effort every second of every game, just like John played the game.

The "$70-per-game" players did not live up to Coach Ritter's high standards. But, unlike Bob Knight and Norman Dale, Coach Ritter was "soft spoken".

There was at least one instance in which he wasn't soft spoken. John was ejected from a game against the Lafayette Lasers for receiving three consecutive technical fouls. He was more frustrated with the refs than his players. He intended to be whistled for the techs in order to point out the poor officiating. The ALACS won in overtime. A "relieved" Coach Ritter felt the need to issue an apology. "The crowd was just great, I hope they can forgive me."

Unstated disappointment in others may have been a theme running through John's life and personality from his teen years playing on the high school baseball team through his debut as a professional coach. John was "top-notch". He was always "willing to work and hustle". John Ritter was the kind of person that "people can look up to and won't be ashamed to bring their kids to see play basketball." So, why weren't his $75 per game players as committed as he was? Why couldn't they be like Chipper and Ritter?

John Ritter was the type of player that would give everything he had for the team. He'd "leave it all on the court". He'd "give a hundred and ten percent". All the other sports clichés about "laying it all on the line" applied to the effort John Ritter (like Chip Hilton) was known for as a high school and college athlete. It must have been tough for him to understand or accept that others would not pursue excellence and winning with the same zealousness he did.

This difference in expectations between Captain Ritter and his teammates and Coach Ritter and his players, I think, is related to the "distance" classmates and friends experienced with John in social situations. There was a bit of discomfort with John, and in John, because he was operating on an ethical plane "above" everyone else. Later, John would smash this barrier by lowering himself below the rest of us.

After his disappointing experiment with coaching in Anderson, John had a part-time gig as the color commentator for IU and Purdue Basketball games on an Indianapolis television station, WTTV Channel 4. He was replaced after one season by John Laskowski, who was a freshman teammate with John, when John was a senior. "Laz" played on IU's national championship team which had the "perfect season" in 1974-75. John was succeeded by a younger IU teammate from the Bob Knight team that didn't just make it to the semi-finals but actually won the NCAA championship.

I have a very vague memory of seeing John on television commenting on an IU game, but I can't reconcile the time frame. I didn't move to Indy to enter IU Law School until 1977. John's employment with the TV station was during the 1975-76 season. So, it's probably a false memory -- wish fulfillment?

A friend of mine who is a life-long resident of Indianapolis and fanatic IU basketball fan told me that he recalls John looking fit and trim and speaking articulately as the color commentator for Channel 4. Another friend told me that he always tried to catch John on TV, because "he was really good as an analyst of the game." So it's clear that John maintained his athletic good looks, interest in Big Ten basketball, and sharp mind through the mid 1970s.

Next, John sojourned south as an assistant coach for the basketball team at the University of Mississippi.

May 4, 1976
The Delta Democrat-Times *from Greenville, Mississippi, Page 9: Ole Miss hires 3rd coach from Indiana University*

Ole Miss Athletic Director John E. Vaught announced Monday the addition of John Ritter, a three-year starter at Indiana from 1971-73, to the Rebel basketball staff as an assistant coach. The 25-year-old Ritter, who played two seasons under Rebel head coach and then Indiana assistant Bob Weltlich, has been employed since graduation from Indiana in 1973 as a financial analyst for Eli Lilly and Company in Indianapolis, Ind.

The appointment of Ritter was approved Monday by the University's Committee on Athletics and the Board of Trustees of Institutions of Higher learning. A native of Goshen, Ind., where he was an All-State forward in high school, Ritter was a three-year regular for the Hoosiers and served as captain of the 1973 team that finished third in the NCAA finals. A first team Academic All-America (selection in '73), he was drafted by the Cleveland Cavaliers of the National Basketball Association and the Indiana Pacers of the American Basketball Association. At IU, Ritter received the Jake Gimbel Award for athletic and academic excellence and was a two-time Balfour Award Winner for basketball. During the 1976 collegiate basketball season, he served as play-by-play analyst for TVS Sports in its weekly coverage of Big Ten Conference action. Although Ritter will be involved with scouting and recruiting, his primary responsibilities will lie in the area of on the court coaching.

John was on staff at Ole Miss for just two seasons. In pictures with the team he appears quite spiffy, tall and slender in sport coat and tie. John's publicly stated reason for leaving Ole Miss was that he disliked the recruiting part of the job.

Considering the scandals and pressures associated with college recruiting of outstanding high school players, it might not be surprising that the 25-year old Ritter was uncomfortable in that role. Top high school players being recruited by Division I basketball programs were probably more interested in asking what Ole Miss would do for them than what they could do for the university. A selfish me-first attitude would not have set well with our still Chip Hilton-like small-town boy from Goshen.

The Rebels' record of wins/losses while John was on staff was as dismal as the Anderson ALACS. They finished at the bottom of the South East Conference both seasons.

John must have known Coach Weltlich pretty well. Weltlich had been Bob Knight's assistant for the Army team at West Point and came with "The General" to IU. So, Weltlich was on Knight's staff John's junior and senior years.

It is difficult for me to understand how the polite and deferential John Ritter could have gotten along very well with Weltlich (or Bob Knight). Remember the tension revealed in the interview given by John after his last game under Coach Knight -- in which John said he felt relief from pressure now that he was finished playing ball at IU. Weltlich's coaching style was as demanding as Knight's, and he could be just as mean-spirited.

One episode of his aggressive coaching style, foreshadowing criticism levied against him later in his career, followed the team splitting two games in Illinois in 1979; after an all-night marathon bus/plane/bus trip that arrived back on campus on Christmas Day, Weltlich had the team dress for a tape session and practice. (This is described from player Sean Tuohy's point of view in both Michael Lewis' 2006 book **The Blind Side***, pp. 55–56; and Sean and Leigh Anne Tuohy's own 2010 book* **In a Heartbeat, Sharing The Power of Cheerful Giving***, p. 48.) Upon setting up the projector to watch film (at 10 am on Christmas Day), Weltlich leaned into Tuohy's ear and said, "Hey Twelve, Merry Fucking Christmas."*

Wikipedia entry on "Bob Weltlich"

The only way I can make sense of John's decision to stay at IU to be coached by Bob Knight, rather than transfer to UCLA or elsewhere after Lou Watson resigned, was that John's principles required him to stick it out at Indiana because he had made a commitment to the university. Perhaps out of that same sense of loyalty he took the job with Coach

Weltlich at Ole Miss. Still, it's hard to imagine the straight-laced John Ritter we knew in Goshen being comfortable with a coach associating Christmas with the F-word.

That Knight and Weltlich were tough disciplinarians would have set well with the John Ritter we knew in Goshen. But cussing at and abusing players would not. Coach Knight might not have been the terror he became, when he first started coaching at IU. But it didn't take long before he was embarrassing the University with his out-of-control behavior. Knight punched a cop and reportedly shouted obscenities about Puerto Ricans after he was ejected from the 1979 Pan American Games. An arrest warrant was issued but eventually withdrawn. At a Purdue/IU game in 1985 Coach Knight lost his temper and threw a chair onto the court. At a game against Northwestern in 1999, students yelled "Hoosier Daddy" at the IU bench during the game. After IU won in overtime Knight shouted back at them, "Who's your daddy now?!" Before leaving courtside he got into a shoving match with the Wildcats' coach. His erratic and violent behavior continued until he was fired after 29 years as head coach at IU for allegedly grabbing and cursing at an IU student. That incident occurred after Knight was on probation by order of IU President Myles Brand for choking a player.

Accepting or participating in mean, nasty, and abusive treatment of one's "inferiors" doesn't meld with the "Aw shucks" sincerity for which John Ritter was known in Goshen or at Indiana University. Did he finally have his fill of the nastiness after two years playing under Knight and two more years as an assistant under Weltlich? I'm both surprised and dismayed that it took that long for John to realize that "mean people suck".

But what was he to do? Basketball was his life, and the commitment he made to Indiana University had propelled him down this path. The path ended with Coach Weltlich.

-- John became un-stuck --

For the first time John Ritter didn't stick. He quit the job at Ole Miss. John never quit in high school. (The basketball coach supposedly ordered him to quit playing football.) John considered leaving IU after the player revolt against Coach Watson, but he didn't. He stuck. He didn't quit the Anderson semi-pro team. The league went under. John didn't quit the job as color commentator on Channel 4. He was replaced by John Laskowski.

Maybe John was just sick of losing after the Anderson semi-pro debacle and two lousy seasons at University of Mississippi. I can find no record of John Ritter ever speaking harshly or disrespectfully about either Coach Knight or Coach Weltlich. Without John's cooperation to tell his story it is just a supposition that he may have had enough of the Knight-Weltlich hard-ass style of coaching and didn't want to be a part of it anymore. Other factors may have influenced his decision to leave athletics behind and give up on coaching. Family pressures might have drawn him back to Indiana to try to settle into a corporate career at Eli Lilly Co.

The John Ritter we knew in Goshen would stick it out through any commitment he made. The situation with the baseball team, when he left to join the Indiana All-Stars, could be considered an exception. But he was pressured into a Hobson's choice by the IHSAA. Coach Mirer informed me that years later John confessed he regretted that decision and wished he'd stuck with the baseball team.

Remember, "Quitters never prosper!" and all the other inspirational platitudes we were fed by our elders growing up in Goshen. Most of the kids ditched those sentiments during their adolescent rebellion. Perhaps John's grip on the principles underlying those sorts of goody-two shoes mottoes was finally beginning to loosen in his late twenties.

Eli Lilly Co. clearly valued John as an employee, because the company took him back after his aborted coaching career. John resigned himself to being finished with basketball and must have thought he would settle into a career as a corporate executive. His competitive spirit, superior intellect, and natural leadership abilities should serve him well in developing a successful career in business. John could focus on working his way up the corporate ladder to become a senior vice president. That should have been John's next goal, right?

But something was beginning to change within John. In the 2005 article in the *Indianapolis Star* (quoted in Chapter Nine) about ticket scalping, John told the reporter that his troubles had begun when "a divorce and depression sent his life into a tailspin." He told Phil the same thing in 1995, but added "drinking" as another factor. Truthfulness is one of the virtues that are inculcated into a good small-town Midwestern-Protestant upbringing. I've never heard anyone question John Ritter's veracity. But I can't help thinking that John was confusing symptoms with causes.

Quitting the job at Ole Miss in 1978 was evidence that John was beginning to change in significant ways. He was leaving basketball behind for better or worse. The dissolution of his marriage, depression, and excessive drinking would follow. If other reports are credible, John's troubles were even deeper and involved gambling addiction and hanky-panky with company funds. By the end of the 1980s John had fallen into the abyss of isolation and homelessness.

Had the cultural changes that had swirled around him, but seemed not to have touched him, finally affected John Ritter? John implied in the description of his "tailspin" to Phil that his divorce triggered depression and drinking, but I wonder if he wasn't responding to a deeper current. Perhaps John's heart did not leap with joy looking forward to long hours and long years in a suit and tie behind a desk engaged in the corporate politics required to reach the goal of senior vice president. How would that compare to hearing thousands of pumped-up IU fans cheering in Assembly Hall when he ripped off his pinstriped warm-ups to take the court? His goals were so concrete then, to make the play, win the game, end the season at the top of the conference, and make a run in the playoffs. It's easy to imagine that looking forward to an endless stack of reports to review and numbers to crunch might have been depressing.

When John was finally ready to devote himself to a corporate career as a financial analyst, the 1970s were coming to a close. The social-political activism of the 60s had burned out. Introspective navel-gazing was more the national craze in the 70s than protesting social injustices.

Perhaps with playing and coaching basketball behind him, John's commitment to the righteous straight and narrow way began to become un-stuck. Basketball had been so much a part of his life -- player, coach, and commentator. Who was he without it? Had he begun to do some navel-gazing to figure out who he was with athletics no longer the center of his life?

I don't know exactly when John's marriage began to unravel. My guess is that it was probably about the same time in the 1980s as his understanding of who he was also began to unravel.

I wonder whether John ever watched or read Arthur Miller's *Death of a Salesman*. John was still living the American Dream when he settled in to his office at Eli Lilly Co. With a successful business career to look forward to, John could become *The Man in the Gray Flannel Suit*. That was the natural course for him to follow when he was finished with basketball.

Boys who grow up in small towns or out in the rural countryside and love the outdoors and enjoy sports and the honesty of physical labor, well, even as grown men we can't help but look upon a life to be spent working in an office with some amount of dread. Willie Loman (in *Death of a Salesman*) reaches the end of his life and declares that the American dream of grasping for success through ambition, selling, and trying to win every competition was a wasted life. Tom Rath, in Sloan Wilson's *The Man in the Gray Flannel Suit*, doesn't wait until his life is over to admit that fighting his way to the top of a corporate network sucks. He decided a 9 to 5 job, which allowed him time to live, love, and enjoy family, offered a better life than dealing with the constant "cover your ass" of office politics.

Miller's and Sloan's messages and characters were created in the 1950s. But they hit a nerve and rang even more true in the activist 60s and introspective 70s. Maybe that sort of anti-corporate anti-establishment message finally reached John Ritter at some point in the 1980s.

Looking down the long hallway of offices in the Eli Lilly Co. headquarters, and looking up at the many rungs of the corporate ladder he was supposed to climb, did it fire up John Ritter's competitive instincts? Probably for awhile. But, maybe it eventually turned him off. Maybe he finally tuned in and wanted to drop out, like many of his contemporaries from the class of 1969 had done a decade or more earlier.

The former monk and acclaimed author on spiritual topics, Thomas Moore, finds value in the state of depression. He associates depression with a time for the possibility of personal growth and change. From *Care of the Soul: A Guide for Cultivating Depth and Sacredness in Everyday Life*:

Depression grants the gift of experience not as a literal fact but as an attitude toward yourself. You get a sense of having lived through something, of being older and wiser. You know that life is suffering, and that knowledge makes a difference. You can't enjoy the bouncy, carefree innocence of youth any longer, a realization that entails both sadness because of the loss, and pleasure in a new feeling of self-acceptance and self-knowledge. This awareness of age has a halo of melancholy around it, but it also enjoys a measure of nobility.

After giving it his honest effort at the end of the 1970s and through most of the 1980s, the emptiness of corporate life may have caught up with John. Or, John may have been perfectly happy in a suit and tie, until his marriage crashed and his life went into a "tailspin". Whether the divorce was the proximate cause of drinking and gambling, or vice versa, John entered a period of depression by the end of the 1980s. He must have had a gnawing feeling in his gut that the life he was leading wasn't what it was supposed to be. He fled the corporate-business life to be alone in his cab.

For at least five years John was depressed and alone with his cab. During that period of desolation he acquired the self-acceptance and self-knowledge that he could recreate himself without basketball, without a Fortune 500 corporate job, and even without his marriage.

John told Phil in 1995 that he was dealing with depression and a drinking problem. That he was able to talk to a sympathetic stranger about his life and the issues he was coping with is evidence that John had already hit bottom and was beginning the difficult ascent out of the darkness.

Phil didn't tell me whether John evinced any joy when Phil tossed him a basketball to play a game of HORSE in Phil's driveway. I imagine "a halo of melancholy" (Moore, above) around John as he held the ball in his big hands and contemplated taking the first shot. When John released the ball and it arced toward the basket I wonder if he felt some relief from the pressure that had pushed him over the edge. Perhaps he even felt a moment of "the bouncy, carefree innocence of youth" playing ball again. Phil did say that he saw both sadness and kindness in John's eyes -- "a measure of nobility"?

John's life departed from the road he had been traveling. He took a road less traveled when he left the security of a job and home. John would have to find out who he was detached from all his successful accomplishments. To escape being John Ritter, the All-Star and junior executive on his way up, he would have to "leave it all on the court" in an entirely different way.

Whatever were the interwoven relationships of

depression, divorce, drinking, and gambling, John spent the first half of the 1990s coming to terms with those challenges. By the end of that decade, John Ritter was a different person. He had been homeless. His figure devolved from an all-star athlete. He lost his hair and some of his teeth. And, he drove a cab instead of sitting behind a desk at a Fortune 500 company.

By dropping out of the race for corporate success, John Ritter was once again out of step with the culture. Because the 1980s and 90s were the go-go Reagan-Clinton Years, the Me Generation, and Yuppies. We were supposed to be materialistic in the 80s and 90s. Enough with cultural revolution and meditation, the Rat Pack was back in style. It was cool to be greedy.

John Ritter gave corporate life a go in the 1970s and 80s. He had played the game fair and square. He had stuck to his principles. He hadn't become a pro ball player or succeeded as a coach, but he was reaping the rewards of the system to which he had been loyal. He had remained true to the Chip Hilton ideals he exemplified when he slapped a nine-year old kid on the back and said, "Great game, Rasley!"

But then, he let go of the ladder. By the 1990s John truly ceased to be John Ritter, the golden boy of Goshen, Indiana. So, who would he be when he emerged from the abyss and he could honestly say by 2001 that he was not John Ritter anymore?

Chapter Fifteen

Rebirth

Who a person is in the full complexity of human being is a question that cannot ever be fully answered. I don't claim to understand fully the essence of John Ritter. A collage of incidents in his life and guess work about his personality and motives, based on imperfect recollections, is the result.

A final article helps to sum up much of what I learned about John Ritter's life after the player revolt at IU during the 1970-71 season.

The Courier-Journal
College basketball news for Kentucky, Louisville and Indiana from courier-journal.com 29 July 2002
While IU officials don't condone it, Ritter says working as a ticket broker is fun. "The phone rings constantly, and so it's fast-paced. I'm happy doing this."
It's game night, and thousands of fans have converged on Assembly Hall in Bloomington, Ind.
Those who don't have tickets to watch the Indiana University basketball team often congregate outside the north lobby.
John Ritter, who was a starting forward on Bob Knight's first Final Four team at IU and once outscored Notre Dame's entire squad, is scalping tickets near the arena he used to play in.
He fell into this line of work after a bout of depression following a divorce. But don't feel sorry for him.
Once down and out, Ritter claims that selling tickets isn't just his livelihood. He said it helped turn around his life. When Renny Harrison, his boss and co-owner of Circle City Tickets, asked for Ritter's help almost a decade ago, it was Ritter's ticket to a fresh start. He has been doing this full time for the past four years.
But Ritter is most visible when he is on the street. And the chances of him being recognized increase when he is standing outside Assembly Hall.

"When I first started doing it, it felt a little strange," he said. "When I was in school I never realized that (scalping) went on. But I talked to people who say it did. It really doesn't bother me at all. Occasionally I would see Coach Knight after a game and I'd shake his hand. I'm not sure what he thought about it."

Steve Downing, a former IU associate athletic director and teammate of Ritter, went a step further when interviewed prior to accepting a job at Texas Tech.

That was notable since Knight didn't recruit him and because Ritter called playing for Knight "stressful". After a standout career at Goshen (Ind.) High School, Ritter went to Bloomington to play for Lou Watson.

Watson was an offensive-minded coach whose philosophy was to outscore the opponent, an appealing style for Ritter. And while Ritter said he didn't enjoy the workmanlike approach, his career took off. His shooting ability, smarts and ability to work off screens and draw fouls connected with IU's new offense. Ritter, a three-year starter, averaged 14.3 points and shot 50.4 percent over his final two seasons.

"John wasn't tremendously talented as a player, but he was one of those guys who would run through a wall to win a basketball game," Downing said.

Ritter helped lead the Hoosiers to the 1973 Final Four. The team finished 22-6 and won the Big Ten Conference championship in Knight's second season. "John was a perfect player for Knight," said Baylor coach Dave Bliss, a former IU assistant.

After his playing days were over, Ritter seemed to take the first step to a promising future. The academic All-American landed a job as a financial analyst at Eli Lilly in Indianapolis. He also stayed close to college basketball, working as a television color commentator. Ritter became even more entrenched in basketball when he accepted a position as an assistant coach at Mississippi. Bob Weltlich, who tutored Ritter as an assistant under Knight, had just been hired to coach the Rebels and was looking for help.

Ritter, however, left in 1978 after two seasons, saying he didn't like recruiting. He returned to Eli Lilly, this time as a corporate credit manager. He later took the same position at another company and worked as a credit manager for seven years before his life took a dramatic change. After 14 years of marriage, Ritter went through a divorce, which he said led to a long period of depression. His ex-wife, Sarah, did not return a phone message. But Ritter, a father of three, said that he "did not handle the situation well."

In 1991 Ritter says he quit a job that paid between $60,000 and $70,000 annually. He eventually took a job driving a cab that paid $300 weekly. For the next three years, Ritter was a cab driver adjusting to a different kind of life. He said there were times he was so financially strapped that he didn't have a place to live. He often would get a cheap hotel room for the night.

"I kind of gave up on life," he said. "I wasn't so depressed that I wanted to kill myself. But I just didn't want to be around people. I just gave up. Coach Knight would not be very happy with that (attitude). But I didn't know what to do."

Ritter said he could have changed his situation but didn't have the will to do so until he met Harrison, a 21year-old IU student, outside Assembly Hall at a basketball game in 1993. Harrison recognized Ritter, and the two struck up a conversation. Harrison said he needed help picking up and delivering tickets.

For the first time in a long time Ritter said he felt needed. "He didn't say, 'Let me help you,'" Ritter said. "He said, 'I need some help selling tickets. Do you have any time?'"

Ritter initially worked part time for Harrison while doing some freelance accounting work. But as the years went by he became more involved. In 1998 he started working for Harrison full time and says he makes as much money now as he previously did. According to Harrison, Ritter now basically runs the office.

"He has made enormous differences in the lives of the owners here," Harrison said. "He's exceptionally smart. I am amazed every day at how aware he is and how he can read people. His involvement has given us the freedom to not be here every minute of every day."

Still, not everyone is happy that Ritter has chosen this line of work. A number of IU officials are aware of Ritter's presence and wish he wouldn't sell tickets outside of Assembly Hall.

But Ritter sees himself as a businessman providing a service and helping bring joy into people's lives -- much as he did as a *player.*

The ***Courier-Journal*** article was published in 2002, so we might wonder whether the portrayal of John is still accurate. The evidence indicates John's life is even better now. He still works at Circle City Tickets. According to the article his full-time employment with CCT began in 1998, so he's been with CCT for eighteen years as of 2016. Phil told me that when he last talked with John, which was about the time I began writing this book in the Fall of 2015, John was still happy working there. Phil also said John "looked older" than his then 65 years and that there was still "a sadness in his eyes". But John was, as always, "polite, friendly, and he seemed content."

Another friend who has bought tickets from John at CCT tells me that John is a little heavy, but he wouldn't call him obese. That John is still honest as the day is long. "If John doesn't have the best deal on tickets for me, he tells me where to find the best price."

It's tempting to slip back into idealizing John Ritter in a very different way than my 9-year old self did. When I spoke with John he didn't try to deflect my questions. He was humble and genuine. He truly thought no one would be interested in reading about him. Seems he's retained the shy and self-effacing aspect of his personality described by his high school classmates.

The fact that John did not want to be interviewed for this book, because he wants to protect his family, shows that he cares more about his children and grandchildren than trying to grab the spotlight one more time. He insisted that, if he was to tell his own story, it would have to be the whole truth. This reflects a moral character once again guided by the principles of honesty and truthfulness, but now leavened by several years attending a school of hard knocks.

John Ritter bears little resemblance to Dennis Rodman, but like Rodman, John would not claim to be anyone's role model; but for the opposite reason of Rodman's. He was and is too humble and honest about himself to make that claim. But now, John's modesty is earned. It's no longer that of a dutiful Boy Scout. He has gained true humility at the cost of losing himself as the sports star and perfectly behaved role model he was at Goshen High, IU, and Lilly. He's older and wiser, but has returned to a similar value system of his youth. Liberated from the pressured expectations, of himself and others, to fulfill the role of Chip Hilton-like perfection, John has, in a way, come full circle.

He's no longer an athlete and he's not coaching, but the career he has developed as a ticket broker is related to sports. As Phil reported to me, John is in a pretty good place in life. He's "providing a service and helping bring joy into people's lives -- much as he did as a player."

John was lost but eventually found a new self. But that's not quite the end of my John Ritter hero story.

Jeff Rasley

Chapter Sixteen

The Hero's Journey Home

Joseph Campbell declared in his first magnificent and sprawling work on cross-cultural mythology and comparative religion, **The Hero with a Thousand Faces**, that he had discovered archetypal stages of the hero's journey. Campbell explains that certain commonalities emerged from his worldwide study of ancient and modern myths, legends, fairy tales, art, and literature as to what a character must accomplish and endure to become a "mythical hero".

Campbell's description of a mythical hero who has made the Hero Journey differs somewhat from the definition of *hero* in **Google Dictionary** and the way the term has been used so far in this book. We've mainly considered what it means to be a hero in our contemporary culture and how the meaning has changed and is changing. The qualifying factors I've identified, which make a hero, can be summarized as:

1. Deeds have been performed that are extraordinarily beneficial to someone (a personal hero), the community (local hero), nation (national hero), or world (international hero).

2. The accomplishment was so impressive and appreciated that it is remembered by witnesses and beneficiaries, and they feel compelled to report it to others.

3. Fame at some level is established.

4. The identity of the hero and his accomplishments become associated with positive values or virtues.

5. The hero as representative of valued principles becomes a figure of inspiration to other people. (As an example, when we think of Louis Pasteur, it conjures up the image of the creative, hard-working scientist-physician. He was an example and is now a symbol of the modern scientist-healer. His development of pasteurization and vaccinations

changed the world. Pasteur is an inspiration to current medical researchers who follow his historical lead in using science-based medicine to improve healthcare and standards of living. The fireman who saved your cat, when you were a child, will always be remembered and associated in your mind with virtues like Courage and Compassion. You'll enjoy telling the story at family gatherings the rest of your life about your personal hero.)

    6. If reports about the hero and his deeds are passed on to future generations, so that he achieves historical significance, then he becomes a historical hero.

    7. History and what a culture values may change, so one who was a hero may later be considered something less, or even a monster. (E.g., General Nathan Bedford Forest and Cecil Rhodes, above, or an even more extreme example would be Adolph Hitler. The German people loved him as their Fuhrer, but now most Germans look back with shame on his monstrous deeds.)

    Joseph Campbell was not concerned with actual historical heroes. What he was interested in were the stories that were generated about the great characters in oral traditions which evolved into myths, legends, fairy tales, or sacred literature. He wasn't defining *hero* per se. Campbell's intention in **The Hero with a Thousand Faces** was to share the stories he discovered and to pull out of them the common narratives and the typical characters that people the stories, such as gods, kings, queens, knights, maidens, prophets, healers, witches, etc., but especially heroes. Out of the morass of stories Campbell collected, his students and readers can discern certain stages through which mythical heroes from all sorts of different cultures pass. These stages form the sequence of the archetypal journey of the mythical hero.

    Campbell's heroes are the figures that have become associated with cultural archetypes. They are characters that have transcended history. Moses, Achilles, Buddha, Jesus, Lancelot and Arthur are examples well known in Western culture. But hero stories from sources and cultures as diverse as the American Plains Indians, Celtic tales, German fairy tales, sacred Hindu literature, and many more are reviewed in **The Hero with a Thousand Faces**. Campbell claimed to find common stages of the Hero Journey in stories from every ancient and indigenous culture.

There are interesting parallels between the journey of the mythical hero and the lives of many of our historical and contemporary heroes. The heroes of history, literary fiction, and our personal heroes need not have made the journey Campbell requires of mythic heroes to merit being called Hero. But the course of the lives of some of these heroes closely tracks the mythical Hero Journey.

The story of John Ritter that I have pieced together, to a remarkable degree, follows the major markers on the journey Campbell describes. John's life has unfolded in ways remarkably similar to the Hero Journey.

Students of Campbell have drawn up lists and diagrams of the stages or phases of the Hero Journey extracted from the master's meandering magnum opus. There is some disagreement among Campbell disciples about the sequence of the stages of the Journey and what to call the different stages, because the book is such a mash up of stories from all over the world spanning thousands of years. But the sequence of meaningful experiences of the Hero Journey Campbell describes, as I discern them, which correspond to John Ritter's life, are: John responded to *The Call* to be the (athletic) *Representative of his Community*. He had *Mentors*; the coaches *who helped him along the way* to become a star player. John faced and passed many *Tests and Challenges* to become Goshen's best basketball player and *the Champion of his community*. But then, he *fell into an Abyss to die* a metaphorical death by the loss of his identity as a star athlete, corporate executive, and head of his family. To climb out of the abyss he had to be *Reborn* with a new sense of who he is. John was

Transformed; he was no longer "that John Ritter". He is the John Ritter who is a valued member of the Circle City Tickets team. He is the John Ritter who has reunited with the family he deeply cares about.

The final stage of the hero's journey, according to the Campbell schema, is that he either *Returns Home* or begins a *New Journey*. A final condition is that the hero brings home a *Magic Elixir* that will heal his suffering community. Or, the hero will take the elixir elsewhere as he embarks on a new journey.

> *There is a road, no simple highway*
> *Between the dawn and the dark of night*
> *And if you go no one may follow*
> *That path is for your steps alone*
> **Ripple**, lyrics of the Grateful Dead)

The Dead's lyrics paint a picture of that lonesome highway the hero must travel. At some point, he must go it alone and survive the dark night of the soul. If he does, then there is the possibility of rebirth. But in the Campbell schema, even after a transformative rebirth the hero must suffer through an *atonement* and then *rapprochement with his community*. A further price is still to be paid after the hero emerges from the abyss reborn into a new day.

Most of us have experiences which are like many, or all, of these stages in our own life journey. Joseph Campbell concedes that the stages of the hero journey he describes are offered to each of us by virtue of our very existence as conscious human beings. But we modern folk, Campbell contends, have lost touch with the meaning of the stages of our journey, because the rationalization-modernization-commercialization of our lives has alienated us from the existential poetry and mythic quality of life.

Still, even us existentially-wretched moderns know what it's like to face and overcome challenges with the help of mentors. Many of us have felt, at some point in our lives, bereft of community and kinship. Some have, and probably more wish we could, shed an old no longer functional identity. Who among us hasn't willingly, or by compulsion, paid for our mistakes and atoned for the sins we've committed? And, there's nothing sweeter than being welcomed home into loving arms after a long and harrowing travel adventure, especially when we bring back presents for our loved ones.

Living a full life with its ups and downs and all the struggles we go through to transition through the different stages of life from infancy through old age unto death -- that can look a lot like Campbell's Hero Journey. If you feel the meaning of life deep in your bones, and, after gaining wisdom through trials and tribulations, you return to your community to mentor the young, then you have approximated the hero's journey. But the masses (in Campbell's view) who live superficially and don't experience or understand the deep significance of the stages of life they pass through -- they have not made the hero's journey no matter what they do with their lives.

What the hero accomplishes is far greater than earning a gold watch for thirty years of faithful service. What the hero suffers is far worse than the pain of loss from divorce or the deaths of loved ones -- these are terribly painful but they are experiences which occur in the ordinary course of life.

We might reasonably call living through and vanquishing the demons of alcoholism, drug addiction, sexual abuse, and other traumas *heroic*. A person who conquers those demons or other terrible temptations might be worthy of praise. But a hero is more than praiseworthy. A hero is larger than life. A hero has lived an extraordinary life by the way he has volunteered to take up the challenge to fight the dragon for his community; has in some sense died to complete the trial set for him by fate; and then almost miraculously been reborn to bring home some power to help restore his suffering community.

    Louis Zamperini is a modern hero whose life's journey took him through most of Campbell's stages. Zamperini's story has become widely known through the best selling biography, ***Unbroken: A World War II Story of Survival, Resilience, and Redemption***, by Laura Hillenbrand (Random House, 2010) and the 2014 movie, *Unbroken*, directed by Angelina Jolie.

    Zamperini ran the 5,000 meters race in the 1936 Olympics as a track star for the US. In 1943 he was the bombardier of a B-24 Liberator bomber, which crashed into the Pacific Ocean during a mission. Louie and surviving crewmates drifted for 47 days on a raft before capture by the Japanese. He spent the rest of World War II as a POW. Louie survived horrible tortures devised to humiliate and break him by a sadistic camp commander. After his release and return home, Louie tried to resume his career as an elite distance runner with the goal of returning to the Olympics. The injuries he suffered from torture during his internment doomed his efforts. He became an alcoholic, suffered from PTSD, and nearly ruined his marriage. Zamperini was inspired by hearing Billy Graham preach. He became a Christian and devoted the rest of his long life to work with the YMCA and reconciliation between the US and Japan.

    Louis Zamperini's story is a journey from glorious conquests as an athlete to a hellish endurance of torture and despair to rebirth in Christian commitment and then mentoring the young and serving others through the YMCA. Louie died at the age of 97 just after *Unbroken* was finished but before its release. As his story spreads, Louis Zamperini is becoming a legend who represents Indominantability, Courage, Compassion, and Reconciliation.

    Now, you might think I have ridiculously aggrandized John Ritter into something he is not. How can I compare his life and achievements with, say, Louis Zamperini? Other than his basketball skills and SAT score, is John Ritter really any more extraordinary than the rest of us? Yes, and no.

I am not trying to mythologize John Ritter. He's not a mythical hero or legendary character. At this point in his life, he might even be characterized as just a decent fellow who survived a rough patch. Most of his troubles were self-inflicted.

On the other hand, John has lived an exceptional life, in part, because his athletic and academic abilities raised him above the crowd. But he is also intriguing because his life did not go according to the plan for which he seemed so well suited. Why did one so talented, admired by peers, and showered with awards and recognition by the world break off from the path he seemed destined to follow to go down a road less traveled?

John began to weave off course when the player revolt against Coach Watson occurred in 1971. His life was completely off the rails by the time he drove Phil home from the airport in 1995. John Ritter, the golden boy from Goshen and IU basketball star, had died a metaphorical death by the time he turned his back on Dean and disappeared into the anonymous darkness. He's not a national or historical figure, but John's life journey, as a local hero, is passing through the stages of the Hero Journey Campbell describes.

-- *Successful but not heroic* --

Some outstanding athletes, and other extraordinarily gifted people, follow what seems a predestined path to success. For some people, outstanding accomplishments just seem to come naturally and easily. Nature and nurture in rare but occasional cases form an alliance to create a person who seems perfectly suited to fulfill a destiny of greatness. These gifted individuals never fall off the ladder or deviate from their destiny.

One of my son Andrew's childhood friends, Eric

Gordon, was blessed with the DNA of very athletic, loving, and caring parents. At seven years-old Eric was recognized as a gifted athlete. He left behind the school teams and recreational leagues in which his classmates were playing to join elite private teams with professional-quality coaches. It paid off. Eric was named Indiana's "Mr. Basketball" his senior year in high school. He played one year at IU and has been playing in the NBA ever since. Eric's life is not tracking the Hero Journey; at least not yet. He is fulfilling his destiny and overcoming the challenges life has created for him. Of course things could change, but at present no Abyss yawns before him. Eric might be living through the stage of conquering hero, but it seems unlikely that he will forsake his identity in the future. He is a popular and good guy, as well as a terrifically talented basketball player. At this stage of his life journey, his success looks like it will continue on beyond the end of his basketball career.

    Despite his manifest character flaws, Donald Trump seems like he knew he was meant for greatness (please liberal Democrats and Trump haters bear with me) and has achieved it in his own terms. His run for the US Presidency might be his first "huge" (everything about The Donald has to be titanic) defeat. I am typing these words during the early Presidential Primaries. Some pundits still believe Trump's bid for the Presidency is a lark or long-running commercial for the Trump brand. So, even a loss might be another business success for him.

    What ever you think about Donald Trump, we all know a person about whom it's remarked, "Some guys get all the breaks." Trump was blessed with a rich father who staked The Donald to give him a leg up in the commercial real-estate-development business. That initial break combined with Trump's drive and business savvy have made him the billionaire name brand that he is. By his own definition, if not yours, he is great. But his life is not the Hero Journey.

    A true hero does not get all the breaks. He must be

willing to lose himself in order to save his own, or some other, community. The hero dies a metaphorical death and is resurrected like the Phoenix -- out of loss and through atonement are the boons of courage, wisdom, and compassion won. The hero's journey is one of loss as well as victory. The hero is a winner and a loser.

-- John Ritter's journey --

Except for his working class roots, John Ritter looked like one of those guys who got all the breaks. His DNA gave him the physical traits of a natural athlete. Genes and a proper Midwest upbringing helped him develop the mental capacity to make As in school and the smarts to win games on the playing fields. A winning personality made him teachers' and coaches' pet. His life was set on a course assured of reaching the higher rungs of success in society. If he failed to make an NBA team, John had all the tools needed to do whatever he wanted, whether he came back home to Goshen or set out for greener pastures in a big city. The IU Athletic Department would surely offer him a job or open doors for him, as it did for Steve Downing, to launch a career in coaching or athletic administration. For god's sake, John was an Academic All-American as well as one of the best basketball players to don the Hoosiers' Cream and Crimson pinstripes. He had it made whatever route he wanted to take after college.

John started down the established route by coaching, being a sports color-commentator, and then an exec at a big company. But John eventually left all of the paths to success and forsook all of the opportunities that his gifts and hard work had opened up for him. He stopped taking advantage of what he had been given through the blessings of nature and nurture, as well as the connections he'd made along the way. He let go of the ladder he had been climbing to achieve the rewards promised for his dedication and effort.

The hero's path is not strewn with roses nor is it paved

with gold. A dragon awaits the hero. He must fall into the Abyss and die before he can be reborn. Even then, he must make atonement before he can return home.

Donald Trump doesn't qualify as a hero, in Joseph Campbell's terms, because Trump (according to Trump) never loses. He's never fallen into the Abyss. He has never been Reborn. He is the king of Trump Tower and sits on his throne surrounded by framed pictures of himself receiving his deserved rewards. He has lived an extraordinary life and he might be envied for his billions, his chutzpah, fame, his three serially beautiful wives, or his hairdo. But his life's journey is more like that of a king, not a hero.

A hero must suffer. The guy who always wins is like John Calvin's Elect. The Elect in Calvinist-Presbyterian theology are chosen by God, not because they deserve to go to Heaven, but just because they were lucky enough to be chosen by God. Some people win the birth Lottery and are born aristocrats. If they don't screw up, life is a bowl of cherries.

John Ritter was born with the right genes and supportive environment to become a basketball star and outstanding student. He was given the help along the way to actualize his potential, and he worked hard at his craft. But when he didn't achieve the success he and his hometown expected, it was like a surprise discovery that he was not among the Elect. The road ahead for John must have become increasingly obscure. There was no clear path and then the Abyss yawned before him.

If he has found his way back onto the upper road in life, then John Ritter has travelled most of the Hero's Journey described by Joseph Campbell. The trials and challenges John has faced are ones a perennial winner like The Donald will probably never know.

The final stages of Joseph Campbell's 12-step program of hero recovery require *Atonement for a Return to Community* or, alternatively, to *Continue the Journey*. The hero must find *The Elixir* his community needs for its own healing, and then bring it home. But, if the community is unworthy or unwilling to accept its need for healing, then the hero may take the elixir to some other place where it is needed.

John Ritter has reached a place in life where most of the major obstacles and transformative experiences are behind him. If he has atoned for his failings, then he is ready to find and bring home the elixir. Or, maybe he already has; because maybe, his hometown was unworthy and he has found another community that has already accepted his elixir.

The rejection of John by the Goshen Chamber of Commerce must have felt like a hard push toward, or back into, the abyss. His period of depression and homelessness was the Abyss. When he was driving a cab to survive ("I had to drive or die"), that was the beginning of his struggle to climb out of his abyss. Picking up extra bucks as a ticket scalper and then getting hired by Circle City Tickets must have felt transformative. I'll bet it felt like being born again, when he had a regular place to live and a job he liked waiting for him each morning.

I don't know whether John interpreted scalping tickets outside of IU and Pacer games as a form of atonement. It must have felt very weird at first for John to be barking out the price of his tickets, hoping to sell admission into arenas where he had performed with such grace and élan as a star player and later as a TV color-commentator. Willing to suffer that humiliation is, I think, more worthy to qualify as atonement or penance than the pro forma recitations of the "Our Father" or "Hail Mary" required by Roman Catholic priests in the confessional. Whatever John might think, I think he has purified himself and is ready to come home to Goshen.

-- What is the magic elixir? --

According to my Goshen sources, John has refused all invitations to come back to Goshen to accept the accolades deserving of a local sports hero. The right time for John to return to Goshen, if ever, is for him to determine. If he does come home, his journey as a hero will be complete according to the Campbell schema, so long as he brings the elixir.

What elixir might John have for Goshen? Campbell refers to the elixir as the hero's "life-transmuting trophy" (Campbell, p. 193). John already sent home the trophies of a high school and college sports star. At this stage in his life there are few, if any, trophies to be won. Perhaps the trophy/elixir is a message or lesson.

Another description of the elixir Campbell uses is "the runes of wisdom" (Campbell, p. 193). I think John has a message/lesson about redemption for his home town gained from hard-earned wisdom. That's what I told John when we talked about his story on the phone.

Joseph Campbell put it this way. After rebirth, the hero's "second solemn task ... is to return then to us, transfigured, and teach the lesson he has learned of life renewed" (Campbell, p. 20). John has certainly been transfigured from the graceful teenager that left Goshen in 1969. And, he surely must have wisdom that he could offer, which he's gained by living through and reflecting on his successes, failures, and rebirth.

Henry David Thoreau retreated to Walden Pond. He'd reached a point in his life that, like John, he just didn't want to be around people. The folly of ambitious striving and spending a life working to win the praise of others were themes he obsessed upon and run through **Walden**, the literary product of Thoreau's retreat into the woods. He emerged from a two-year period of introspective isolation with a renewed commitment to his art and working for social justice and the abolition of slavery. Surely John Ritter also plumbed the depths of his own soul during his self-imposed exile at night alone in his cab. What themes obsessed him while he worked through his existential crisis to emerge a different John Ritter?

The mass of men lead lives of quiet desperation. ... But it is characteristic of wisdom not to do desperate things.

The greater part of what my neighbors call good I believe in my soul to be bad, and if I repent of anything, it is very likely to be my good behavior. What demon possessed me that I behaved so well? (**Walden or Life in the Woods**, Henry David Thoreau, Signet Classics, printed 1999, p. 7 & 9)

The perfect boy from Goshen ceased playing that role and became bad. He turned his life upside down to be released from the pressure of always behaving so well. He committed all the sins he'd seen, or heard about, his high school and college friends engage in, while he had maintained his own upright integrity. The boy who never smoke, drank, or cussed became a binge drinker, gambler, and worse. But then, he left that life and those vices behind to retreat into his own Walden. He retreated from family, friends, and community for a period of years living in relative isolation. He must have pondered who he wanted to be and how he wanted to live before he began to emerge from this cocoon-like stage in his life. Instead of the easy and orthodox platitudes offered as wisdom for boys in the **Chip Hilton Sports Series**, what Thoreau-like wisdom did John Ritter gain from his period of exile from community?

John Ritter has stood higher and felt lower in life than most of us. His six foot five inch frame, superior intellect, athletic ability, and self-confidence gave him an advantage that only a tiny fraction of the human population will experience. His fall into an abyss is, perhaps, not such an uncommon experience. We all know people who have screwed up a good life with alcohol, drugs, crime, divorce, gambling, etc. But those few who have achieved extraordinary heights of glory and made it through the darkest and loneliest night of the soul to be reborn -- if they can come back home transformed into wiser and better people, they must have something almost magical to offer the rest of us. If you can touch the heavens, descend into your own hell, and survive to continue your journey, you surely have something special to give back to your community.

Exactly what lesson could John Ritter teach his old fans back in Goshen now? What might he be able to say in 2016 or 2017 to a 9-year old kid wearing a baseball cap looking up into John's older and sadder, but wiser, blue eyes? I wish he had told me.

-- Redemption of the suffering community --

John was still involved with the community of Goshen for a period of time after his IU playing days ended. He played in charity games for the Goshen Stars against the County Stars to raise money for the March of Dimes in 1973 and 1974. The local stars from Goshen played basketball against their counterparts from around Elkhart County "before capacity crowd" and raised $3,187 in the 1973 game, according to a Facebook post by former **Goshen News** Sports Editor Stu Swartz about historical local sporting events in Elkhart County. John Ritter led the scoring with 39 points.

John's involvement with his hometown probably began to decline when he left Indiana for the coaching job at Ole Miss. I don't know to what extent, if any, he visited Goshen after his return to Indiana to begin employment with Eli Lilly Co. His parents still lived in the Goshen area until the death of John's father in 1989. His mother moved at some point after that to nearby Angola, Indiana, where she resided until her death in 1999.

The good community that raised him up should not have rejected and refused to deal with John when he came home asking for a job. Goshen has changed dramatically from the 1960s when John thrilled Redskins fans with his feats on the court and made the grades needed for induction into the National Honor Society. Its population has tripled since John patted me on the back. Its demographics and culture are significantly altered by the influxes of Appalachian and

Hispanic migrants. But its "ruling class" still includes some of the same WASP families that cheered for John in high school and college. Their fathers, the patriarchs of the community, could have found him a job when he needed help. They didn't. The community owes him.

On the other hand, John might choose not to come back to Goshen ever again. He doesn't have any family left in Goshen. It would be asking a lot of him to forgive the rejection of the Chamber of Commerce. "The return and reintegration into society ... which, from the standpoint of the community, is the justification for the long retreat, the hero himself may find the most difficult requirement of all." (Campbell, p. 36)

If John is honored by the Elkhart County Sports Hall of Fame and recognized by Goshen High School at his 50th class reunion in 2019, healing could begin. Alternatively, he could be named honorary grand marshal of the 4-H or Labor Day Parade, like he was by Putnam County when he graduated from IU in 1973. He could also be granted an honorific award by the Chamber of Commerce or given the key to the City by Goshen's mayor. By granting John Ritter recognition as the hometown hero he was, and is, Goshen could redeem itself for failing him in a time of need. As Campbell puts it, "the boon (referring to the elixir) may redound to the renewing of the community ..." (Campbell, p. 193).

I'm not suggesting John Ritter should be honored by his hometown just because I think the Chamber of Commerce wronged him over twenty-five years ago. He qualifies for special recognition because he is one of the most outstanding citizens that grew up in the Goshen area and graduated from Goshen High School. I don't know of any other graduate of Goshen High in my lifetime, with the possible exception of Rick Mirer, who won as many awards as John did for athletic and academic excellence. And, I wouldn't shrink from recognizing the altogether different path from local expectations John's life has taken. His many awards for integrity and as a scholar-athlete are testament to John as an example of personal excellence. The rest of his life is a lesson in the great American tradition of rebounding from failure. John's rebirth should be celebrated right along with his achievements in this land of second chances.

But maybe Goshen is no longer John Ritter's home town in any meaningful sense. Maybe *Home* is in Indianapolis near his family. Maybe the final phase of his journey is simply spending time with his children and grandchildren. A young grandchild might be that kid with a baseball glove on her hand that John can offer his elixir. The elixir might be the message of grandfatherly love.

Or maybe, working for Circle City Tickets is the new journey John has embarked upon. His fellow employees and customers might be the community to whom he is offering lessons of courage, wisdom, and compassion. According to Renny Harrison, John has brought the boon of sound management and savvy customer relations to CCT.

... Ritter now basically runs the office. "He has made enormous differences in the lives of the owners here," Harrison said. "He's exceptionally smart. I am amazed every day at how aware he is and how he can read people. His involvement has given us the freedom to not be here every minute of every day." (**Courier-Journal** article, July 29, 2002)

John's rejection of my request to interview him for this book could be interpreted as an indication he does not yet believe his atonement is complete. The reason given for the rejection -- John's concern for his children and grandchildren -- I think is evidence that his transformation is complete. He has moved beyond the desire to lose himself in a bottle, and beyond the descent into depression and denial that he is John Ritter. He cares more about his family than telling his story. In this era of narcissism and selfies, giving up any opportunity to be the focus of attention for ethical reasons is admirable.

John has climbed up the slope and out of the abyss to gainful employment. Friends of mine who are acquainted with one of John's children report that there are still difficulties but that wounds within the family are healing and John has participated in family gatherings. If Stu Swartz, Ken Mirer, and other Goshen friends accurately represent the sentiment of the community, then John would be honored and welcomed back into its communal embrace. He could come home to Goshen if he chose to do so. What John could offer to Goshen is his forgiveness, along with his wisdom.

    The journey on which John Ritter embarked, when he set off for IU to fulfill his destiny and the community's expectations for its local hero, I think, is nearing its end one way or another. Not that John is near to death (I hope not, since he is only a few years older than me). Rather, it's because he already has, or will soon, complete the hero's journey and his true existential destiny. He will be complete -- a whole and wise human being -- who can serve as a sage to his family, as well as fellow employees and customers. And he could, if he chose to, redeem his hometown and himself by offering Goshen a lesson in Forgiveness, Courage, Wisdom, and Compassion.

Chapter Seventeen

Final Stage, Redemption from a Tragic Flaw

    When I first read the 2012 *Courier-Journal* article, it summarized much of what I had learned from other sources about John Ritter. So, I wasn't surprised by most of the content. Reflecting back on when I first read the article, what was most unexpected to me was Steve Downing's statement that, "John wasn't tremendously talented as a player ..." What! Goshen's greatest-of-all-time basketball player wasn't "tremendously talented"? Okay, so he wasn't as big, strong, and fast as George McGinnis, or as tall, tough, and dominant as Larry Bird. Ritter fans in Goshen were well aware of his determination to "run through a wall to win a basketball game", but we also thought he was tremendously talented. I certainly did, anyway.

    Bob Knight's less than over-the-top assessment after John's final game for the IU Hoosiers, "His play in *various games* has been outstanding", tracks, I suppose, with Downing's rating of John's talent.

    Maybe it shouldn't be so surprising that the perspectives of professional judges of talent, the college basketball coach that held the record for most career wins and a college athletic director that did play briefly in the NBA, would be different than John's hometown fans. Coach Knight's and Athletic Director Downing's assessments of John's basketball skills are relative to other top Division I basketball players. My awe of John Ritter's talent developed watching John play high school ball. I had never seen someone his age able to do what John Ritter could do with a basketball playing against other high school boys in northern Indiana.

    A friend and fan of John's described John's style of play as "too smooth and deliberate for the NBA". John shot the basketball with picture-perfect form and incredible accuracy. He held the IU record for free-throw shooting percentage for over a decade, until Steve Alford's accuracy proved to be slightly better. John's smooth and deliberate release of the ball was just a little too slow for the hyper-athletic level of play in the NBA, according to sports analysts I've spoken with about why John was unable to earn a roster spot on either the Pacers or Cavaliers.

    Still, I've seen plenty of NBA players that lacked John Ritter's fundamental basketball skill set and his devotion to finding and exploiting the weaknesses of opponents. Why couldn't he have carved a niche for himself on a team that needed a 2-guard or swingman with Larry Bird-like finesse? At 6-5 he wasn't too small for that position. I suppose I have to admit reluctantly that, if John had what it take's to play in the NBA, he would have made it on one of the teams that drafted him.

    Every season, Chip Hilton would encounter at least one other player who out-stripped Chip's ability on the court. In some books it was a new kid who'd moved into town and challenged Chip for a starting position on the team. In others, the boys from Valley Falls would face a Goliath from another town. But grit, intelligent play, and sheer will power, along with the bond of his teammates, created the fabric of excellence which propelled Chip and his team to ultimate victory. Those are the same characteristics Knight and Downing, and his hometown fans, did see in John Ritter.

    But what about the issues with teammates I've raised? Fair point. He was elected co-captain of the high school basketball and baseball teams and the IU basketball team. I think there was significant ambivalence among John's teammates about him. Jack, the disgruntled teammate on the baseball team thought John was "a suck-up more comfortable with the coaches than the players". Some of the guys on the IU Hoosiers must have viewed John in that same light or they wouldn't have ostracized him from the negotiations. On the other hand, John must have been respected for his leadership qualities and personal integrity; otherwise, why would he have been elected captain on each of those teams? "He was the nicest guy around, and could be really funny when guys were hanging around in the locker room," a baseball teammate of John's told me. Almost every high school and college friend of John's I've talked with described a yin and yang to John's personality. He was an exemplary person who you couldn't really get close to.

John really was so much like Chip Hilton. It breaks my heart. If only he had matured in the 1950s, instead of the late 60s and early 70s. Maybe there would have been no ambivalence among his mates. He would have been understood to be exactly the way he should be. His IU teammates would have followed his lead and rallied around Coach Watson. But that's fiction.

-- The fall --

This is where Chip and John, fictional and real person, begin to diverge. Chip Hilton always overcame, by the end of the book, the insecure hostility of the new guy on the team. Chip always found a way to navigate around the conspiratorial intrigues of the rich and envious Fats Olsen. But Chipper didn't succeed solely on his own. His teammates would circle the wagons to protect Chip, when things got hairy. Chip's teammates and coaches, and certainly his doting mother Mary, would never let him fall into an abyss. And that's why John Ritter is more truly heroic, at least in Campbell's terms, than Chip Hilton.

John was admired by just about everybody that ever knew him, from younger kids, to teammates, teachers, coaches, and employers. Yet he also managed to damage or sever relations with teammates, coaches, employers, and family. The incidents with the baseball team and IU basketball team during the revolt against Coach Watson evidenced a flaw, which Chip did not share. It was (to paraphrase The Captain in *Cool Hand Luke*) a failure to communicate. It wasn't that John was inarticulate; rather, he was just out of sync with where other guys were at that time. At critical points in his life John could not, or chose not to, connect with other people in an intimate trusting way. When friends and family should have been there to circle the wagons around him, instead, John was at a place where, "I just didn't want to be around people. I just gave up." (***Courier-Journal*** article)

John identified the beginning of his spiral downward with a difficult divorce. Having handled a couple hundred divorces as an attorney, my guess is that poor communications was a major factor in John's marital problems. It usually is.

When he was depressed and estranged from his family as a consequence of the "difficult divorce", John largely ceased communicating with others. During the homeless cab-driving phase of his life, it was John's choice to cut himself off from people who were willing to hold out a hand of fellowship. I was told by another source who spoke with Bob Knight about John, that Knight made several attempts to reach out to John. Coach Mirer also tried to stay in touch with John and talked to him about "his troubles", but John did not want pity or help. According to Dean, John did ask the Goshen Chamber of Commerce to help him find a job. That might have been John's last ditch attempt to avoid falling into the Abyss before he entered his period of isolation.

I think John cut himself off from family and friends, in part, out of guilt and shame -- guilt for the vices he'd committed and shame that his life was out of control. He may have felt like a failure. He didn't make it in the pros. His career as a sports caster and then as a coach were cut short. Perhaps working at Eli Lilly Co. didn't fulfill him the way athletics had. His marriage failed, and the rumors are that he had gambling debts. At some point he developed a drinking problem. He lost his job with Lilly.

The star of Goshen, Indiana and the IU Hoosiers had fallen from the sky. John must have felt ashamed that he was violating so many of his own standards. To find out who he was, if he was no longer that John Ritter, he must have realized that he needed to isolate himself and atone for his fall from grace.

In the 1990s John Ritter spent several years in a state of depression, occasional homelessness, and battling addictions. John "just gave up" on being in community. He wanted to cut off communications beyond what was necessary to survive. The athlete for whom the whole town cheered, the sharp looking and popular sports commentator, the valued employee of one of the top companies in his home state, "didn't want to be around people". But he would eventually emerge from this swamp of despair a different John Ritter.

-- Rebirth after the fall --

Chip's fictional life never ends. His fans will never learn what his life would be like at age 30, 40, 50 or 60. We can imagine that he would have played pro ball and/or become a coach and wonderful mentor to the next generation of athletes in Valley Falls or at State U. That's the path John Ritter initially embarked upon and his hometown fans expected him to follow. But real life is more precarious and not so nicely predictable.

John Ritter has taken a journey along a very different road than the one I imagined Chipper and Ritter would travel, when they were my childhood heroes. Joseph Campbell had a deeper insight into what is expected of the Hero than Clair Bee had; and a much deeper understanding than I had in my childish innocence.

To be worthy of being called Hero in Campbell's terms, there must be failure and a fall. In John Bunyan's **The Pilgrim's Progress**, the Slough of Despond is a "swamp of despair" to be avoided at all costs on the path of Christian faith. To Campbell, it is unavoidable and necessary on the Hero's Journey.

I know, I know. Campbell is describing the mythical hero's journey, and I am conflating it with a real person existent in my own space-time continuum. But, if you examine the lives of many of our historical and living heroes, you'll recognize a correspondence to the journey Campbell describes. Many did fall into a swamp of despair.

We can quibble over whether he is historical or mythical, but the Gospels depict Jesus in the Garden of Gethsemane as very upset with his disciples and in a state of terrible anguish. Erik Erikson's deeply insightful psycho-biography, *Gandhi's Truth*, claims that the Mahatma struggled with depression and neuroses. Lincoln's gloomy disposition and battles with depression are well documented and poignantly portrayed in the eponymous movie featuring Daniel Day-Lewis. Mother Teresa's private letters released in 2007 revealed that she spent the last fifty years of her life tortured with doubts about her Christian faith. She felt "abandoned by God" and often "empty". Yet, each of these great servant-leaders found a way out of their deep emotional distress to fulfill their calling.

Brett Favre, the record-setting NFL quarterback and hero to Packers fans, is a more contemporary and mundane example. As his NFL career was winding down stories appeared in the news media that he had engaged in Anthony Weiner-like self-porn texting. That was disturbing enough (almost as much as defecting to the hated Minnesota Vikings for the last two seasons of his NFL career), but his sin was compounded in the eyes of his fans by the betrayal of his wife.

Deanna Favre is a breast cancer survivor and activist. She was also a loyal wife and Packers fan. The Favre PR machine represented the Favre marriage as rock solid. But the publication of Brett's depredations must have been devastating to both Deanna and Brett. The marriage had survived an earlier separation. Deanna left and made a condition of reconciliation that Brett deal with his drinking problem.

Deanna was about as popular with Packer fans as Brett on account of her down-home Mississippi ways, courage in dealing with cancer, and ultimately standing by her man through his battles with alcoholism. Brett Favre's reputation was trashed and his marriage had to be in jeopardy when the sexting scandal broke in 2010. Nevertheless, the Favre marriage has survived and, after a hiatus, Brett returned to TV to make jeans and razor commercials. He and Deanna managed to find a way out of what had to be a humiliating and emotionally draining swamp of despair into a renewed life together.

We can debate whether he is a hero or anti-hero, but it's inarguable that Mike Tyson fell into an abyss and has come out the other side. His imprisonment for rape, the crazy-ass biting of Evander Holyfield's ear, and the bizarre facial tattoos were precursors to his fall from grace as an unbeatable champion boxer. Tyson declared bankruptcy in 2003, despite having earned over $300 million from professional fights. He's admitted in interviews to being bi-polar and addicted to cocaine. He's been accused by former wives of physical abuse and serial adultery. In his book and the Broadway show with the same name, *Undisputed Truth,* Iron Mike tells a story of how he found a way out from his imprisonment in uncontrolled anger, emotional torment, and loneliness. He has apologized to Holyfield and others and has become a rather sweet-tempered comedic actor/entertainer.

An incredibly dramatic example of a sports hero that immolated his identity is Bruce Jenner. He was America's hero after winning the decathlon at the 1976 Montreal Olympics. He was perfect! What better hero to feature on the front of the Wheaties cereal box (and later *Playgirl*) than this sculpted floppy-haired guy with a sparkling smile and all-American good looks. He was "the world's greatest athlete" by virtue of winning the Olympic decathlon. His timing was perfect -- to win gold for the US in the Bicentennial Year of 1976. Jenner parlayed his Olympic fame into television and film roles. He was involved in a series of successful businesses in aviation and sports equipment. He even won some races as a race-car driver in the 1980s. Bruce Jenner had it all. Except, he had been hiding a secret; he was really a she in his/her own mind.

Jenner held a renaming ceremony in July 2015, adopting the name Caitlyn Marie Jenner. She appeared on the cover of *Vanity Fair* that same month, and her story was the featured article of the issue, "Call me Caitlyn". Jenner's transformation and coming out as a "trans woman" was a media sensation. According to her entry in *Wikipedia*, Caitlyn Jenner set a Guinness World Record for amassing followers on Twitter surpassing the previous record of United States President Barack Obama. Ms. Jenner describes herself as much more content, since she released herself from the burden of her long-held secret. So far, she seems to be thriving in her new identity.

I could go on. There are many examples of extraordinary men and women who fell into the Abyss at some point in their lives but then managed to claw their way up and out. It is not uncommon in such cases that the survivor describes the experience as "salvation" or being "born again".

It is a transformative journey to descend into an emotional pit, to bottom out, and then struggle back up to the surface. Those who make it through that trial discover what is truly most valuable and meaningful in life. That's why it is so imperative that they bring their wisdom back home or find the appropriate community to share it with.

Some, like Hemingway, Kurt Cobain, and Hunter S. Thompson, don't survive the fall into the abyss. They commit suicide. Think of all the rock stars of the 60s and 70s (and today) that drank and drugged themselves to oblivion and death. It's one thing to groove on the adoration of cheering fans while performing to sold-out stadiums. It's another to deal with the contingencies of life off stage alone in a hotel room during a dark night of the soul.

A case which may strike closer to home for John Ritter is Art Schlichter. The top draft choice by the Baltimore Colts in 1982 (two years before the team was moved to Indianapolis), Schlichter was expected to be a star quarterback in the NFL. He was physically gifted with a rocket arm and the speed and legs of a powerful runner. He failed to live up to the high expectations of NFL fans and coaches. He bounced around for a few seasons before being cut by the Buffalo Bills. He stuck with pro football by dropping down a level. Schlichter led the Detroit Arena League team to a championship and was elected Most Valuable Player of the league in 1990.

Before he took his first snap as a pro football quarterback Art Schlichter was running from demons more fierce than defensive linemen. He had a serious gambling addiction dating back to college at Ohio State. He is currently in prison having been arrested multiple times for illegal gambling, fraud, forgery, theft, and cocaine possession. He was even busted for illegal gambling while he was locked up.

Schlichter's first of many arrests occurred in 1987. He was in and out of jail until January 2012, when he received the most recent sentence of ten years and seven months in federal prison. He owes millions of dollars in restitution orders. In a 2007 interview with ESPN, Schlichter admitted he'd stolen over $1.5 million from friends and acquaintances he'd conned or given bad checks. "He told ESPN that he started gambling because the pressure of being Ohio State's starting quarterback was too much on him, and he wanted to be just a regular guy." ("Art Schlichter" entry, **Wikipedia**) In six years, when he is due to be released from prison, Art should know whether he has managed to climb out of his abyss.

Completing the journey is not for the weak. It takes the strength and fortitude of a hero to make this journey.

-- *A tragic flaw* --

The ancient Greeks' conception of the tragic flaw ("hamartia") provides the explanation, I think, why so many exceptional people fall into an abyss. Hamartia is a character flaw in a hero, which is not, at first, obvious to the hero himself or the hero's admirers. Oedipus in Sophocles's *Oedipus Rex* and Hamlet in Shakespeare's eponymous play are the classic examples of the hero/protagonist with a tragic flaw. In Lit class we learned that Hamlet's tragic flaw was indecision; he just couldn't make up his mind (until he did, and then everyone dies).

"Hubris" is the tragic flaw Literature profs love best. In his book on **Rhetoric**, Aristotle describes certain rich, young men of Athens as "hubristic", "because they think they are better than other people." Hubris is arrogance, but in classic tragedies, it is such spectacular arrogance that it angers the gods and must be punished. It sets up the hero's downfall. The hero thinks he's got the world by the tail, but his fate is sealed because of his hubris, and he doesn't see it coming.

The tragic flaw of the John Ritter character I have tried to capture in this work is a form of hubris. My John Ritter was cursed with perfectionism. John expected others, teammates and the players he coached, to live up to his standards of 1950s moral rectitude, such as sacrifice of self for the team. John was the measure of all things, and those that failed to measure up were not unclean or bad in John's worldview. They were simply baffling to him. But they should rightly expect negative consequences for their failures.

Doesn't that explain why he thought it his duty as a high school team captain to inform on fellow players, as well as himself? Isn't this form of hubris an explanation for John's shock that his IU teammates refused to sign the letter he drafted in support of Coach Watson? Apparently John saw nothing wrong with reporting rule-breaking teammates to the authorities, because that was his duty. He was surprised and disappointed that the other players on the basketball team were unwilling to follow his lead to do the right thing. But, who did he think he was, just a sophomore, telling teammates who were dissatisfied with the coach that they were wrong to express their discontent?

John might have been elected captain of his teams, but his high school classmate, Dean, told me that John wasn't really in the normal society of the class. Another classmate pointed to John's innate shyness and "overly proper" conduct as a reason he wasn't seen as "dating material" by the girls in their class. A teammate, who greatly admired John, remembered his "distance" from the other guys. John's unwillingness to go out with the guys for a brew was one of the reasons John did not intimately connect with others in the "jocks dorm".

John Ritter stood out because he was better than the rest of us. He must have been aware at some level of his consciousness, despite his unassuming demeanor, that he was the only one who lived up to his strict standards. But those who knew him in high school and college did not consider John a judgmental personality. It was more like John was confounded as to why we lesser mortals did not live up to the same level of commitment to proper behavior that he did. He was frustrated that his players on the Anderson ALACS didn't give it their all every minute of every game. This was John's hubris.

I mean, come on, man! Those guys were paid a measly $70 per game, and they're supposed to risk injury and play like their lives depend on winning a basketball game that a couple hundred people turned out to watch? John's expectations of the rest of humanity, and ultimately of himself, were simply too high.

John's demeanor was usually the opposite of arrogant. John Ritter was not just humble, he was kind, courteous, and thoughtful. He was the kind of guy that would make a point of congratulating a younger kid for playing well. His arrogance was not that of a rich, young man that thought he was better than other people. John's hubris was that of the moral perfectionist. He just didn't seem to recognize that his standards of righteous virtue, especially loyalty to authority and sacrifice of self, were not universally accepted by others.

At some point in the 1980s the rigidity of John's moral perfectionism cracked. The creature who was the golden boy finally blew apart under the pressure John had probably felt since junior high school with his father watching his every move at basketball and baseball practice. However it began, drinking, gambling, and other vices must have felt like an incredible release.

It may seem counter-intuitive, if you are a cautious person, but a friend who specializes in therapy for addictive personalities tells me that the gambling addict feels a release of pressure during the high brought on by the excitement of gambling. There is a similar feeling of release for the addictive personality in excessive drinking, drug abuse, or whatever is the particular addictive behavior. She also informed me that, when a star entertainer or athlete can no longer get high off performance and applause, there is a high likelihood that compensation will be sought in sex, drugs, booze, or gambling.

I'm not sure that analysis applies in John's case. Maybe he needed a replacement, or compensation, for the high he felt from his graceful performances on the basketball court and the resulting cheers. But, if that was the case, why did he express relief after his last game as an IU Hoosier? Why didn't he pursue a pro career in Europe, like so many other college stars who didn't make it in the NBA their first try? Why not play in games for the Anderson ALACS when he was player-coach? If he really needed to keep playing for the applause, he could have found ways to do so for awhile. Or, he could have stayed in front of the camera by focusing on a sports announcing career. The reports are that he was good at it.

I think it's more likely that the release John was seeking through his vices of choice was a release of the pressure to be the perfect John Ritter everyone, especially himself, had expected of him for so long. When he finally gave in, John no longer had to be better than the rest of us. He could be worse. The gods had brought down another hero, when John took that first drink or made his first illegal bet.

Whatever relief John gained by giving in to vices, it didn't last all that long. According to the **Courier-Journal** article, John left the corporate world in 1991 and was working at Circle City Tickets by 1998. The depressed and sometimes homeless cabbie Phil met in 1995 was not flying high from gambling, booze, or drugs. John had already left that phase behind. He had bottomed out and was in a fight to see if he could find a way out of his swamp of despair.

By 1995 the stage of John's journey during which he needed to disconnect from other people, as well as his former self, wasn't over but there was light at the end of that tunnel. John recognized his period of alienation from himself and others had ended by the time he could say to Dean that he was not John Ritter anymore.

When Dean first told me about his encounter with John at Deer Creek -- which Dean thinks was in 2001 -- I interpreted John's statement, "I'm not John Ritter anymore", as a terribly sad and disturbing self denial; an indication he was at the nadir of his despair. Having a better sense of the time line of John's journey, I now understand it as John's statement that his rebirth was complete. He wasn't the John Ritter Dean knew in Goshen and IU. John had survived the Abyss and was reborn. A healing process had begun to reconnect with his family. He finally had a steady job at Circle City Tickets.

When hubris catches up with a hero, it will strike him down. Oedipus tore out his own eyes in grief and rage and left his kingdom a blind and lonely exile. John Ritter sat alone in his cab. But he was reborn, like the Phoenix, out of the ashes of his former self into a different John Ritter.

-- Redemption and the Elixir --

John eventually recognized his flaw of being on a different communications frequency than others due to his perfectionism and he has overcome it. He had to be released from the pressure he felt and sink down below regular folks to find his own redemption. He had to recognize and accept his own imperfection. What helped him re-surface was the gift of effective communication with others.

The job of a ticket broker requires the ability to buy and then sell. There is constant interaction with people on both sides of the transaction. John left driving a cab, which can entail fairly minimal conversation, to become a ticket scalper. Scalping is selling, which is talking. When John was ready to begin trying to reconnect with people, he did so by scalping tickets at sports and entertainment events. His skill at that trade eventually led to a regular job as a ticket broker with Circle City Tickets.

John described his work at CCT in the 2012 *Courier-Journal* article thusly, "The phone rings constantly, and so it's fast-paced. I'm happy doing this." The essence of his job as a ticket broker is communicating with others. He has become really good at it. His boss at CCT is quoted in the *Courier-Journal* article: "I am amazed every day at how aware he is and how he can read people." Contrast that with when John was "150%" out of step with his IU teammates. He was so out of touch he didn't realize they wanted changes. He was shocked that his fellows did not support the status quo.

The essential skill in the ability to "read people" is empathy. The reborn John Ritter is not 150% out of step with the people he is dealing with. This John Ritter is aware and in touch with the needs of his clients, colleagues, and employers. The owners have so much confidence in John, he runs the business when they take time off.

Renny Harrison is too young to have been a childhood fan of John Ritter, while John played at IU. The *Courier-Journal* article states that, "he (Ritter) met Harrison, a 21year-old IU student, outside Assembly Hall at a basketball game in

1993. Harrison recognized Ritter ..." If Harrison was 21 in 1993, he was only a year old when John was a senior and co-captain of the Indiana Hoosiers in 1973. So, he must have heard about John from parents, older siblings, or through IU basketball lore.

When Harrison was trying to get a ticket brokerage business off the ground, there stood this mountain of a man outside Assembly Hall scalping tickets on his own. But that huge bald man would be recognized by avid Hoosier basketball fans.

Harrison recognized Ritter, and the two struck up a conversation. Harrison said he needed help picking up and delivering tickets.

For the first time in a long time Ritter said he felt needed.

"He didn't say, 'Let me help you,'" Ritter said. "He said, 'I need some help selling tickets. Do you have any time?'"

What an insightful and exemplary way to throw a lifeline to help pull John out of the slough of despair -- not by offering to help, but by telling John he was needed and offering him work. People I've spoken with who did talk with John during his troubled times each said that John wanted neither pity nor help. Harrison's motives might have been self-serving, but his need of John's talent to sell tickets, to communicate, was just what a wise and sensitive doctor would have prescribed for John. The gods had not forgotten our hometown hero.

The *Courier-Journal* article concludes the way we want our hero stories to end -- with redemptive triumph: "Ritter sees himself as a businessman providing a service and helping bring joy into people's lives -- much as he did as a player."

Chip Hilton is forever young in my mind, still whacking homeruns, throwing touchdown passes, and swishing jump shots. The current picture in my mind of John Ritter is a huge bald guy looming a head taller than the crowd of potential ticket-buyers milling around him outside IU's Assembly Hall. Or, he's slouched in an office chair with a phone cradled to his ear fast-talking a prospective customer while scanning a computer screen. And, he's content.

Chip will never know what it is to marry and have children, and grandchildren. He will never face the challenge of finding the right path to follow when he doesn't make the cut on a pro basketball team and is faced with unfamiliar career choices, like coaching and TV-announcing. He will never experience the depths of emotion John must have suffered as his star faded and he gave in to the temptation of vices. Chip will never descend into despair and loneliness and feel the need to deny that he is Chip Hilton. He will never know divorce or estrangement from family and friends. And, Chip will not know what it means to be reborn, to be saved from the life of a depressed cabbie to gain the new identity of a respected and successful ticket broker and office manager. John Ritter has displayed the strength of will and character of a true flesh-and-blood hero in pulling himself out of the abyss to become a loving father and grandfather, dependable office manager, and caring-communicating human being.

John Ritter stood a head taller than his classmates in Goshen High School. His exceptional talent on the basketball court and in the classroom set him apart. So did his commitment to personal virtue and conformism to traditional values. To younger kids and adults John Ritter seemed about as close to perfect as a boy in Goshen could be.

John sought fame in his sport and was rewarded with being named an Indiana High School All-Star, received a full scholarship to Indiana University, was named an Academic All-American, and drafted by NBA and ABA teams. He was the best of his generation from Goshen in athletics, academics, and personal integrity. John gave us what we prayed for and we praised him for fulfilling the community's need for an example to our youth. But his athletic ability was ultimately not sufficient to fulfill our desire for a star at the highest level. His extreme standards eventually alienated those who should have been his support group. He finally released the pressure that had built in him by violating many of his own fundamental rules. And then, his own community rejected him when he had ceased to fulfill our expectations and had become an embarrassment.

But that was then, and this is now.

John Ritter was an example of courage on the basketball court. As his teammate Steve Downing said, John "would run through a wall to win a basketball game." It took even deeper existential courage to climb out of the abyss of homelessness, isolation, and depression to hold down a job and reunite with his family. My friend Phil tells me there is wisdom behind John's sad but kindly eyes. I haven't yet seen it, but I believe it.

John's decision not to grant interviews for this book, because a commitment to truth would require telling "the whole story", which might be detrimental to relationships within his family, reveals integrity and compassion. John values truth and he loves his family. It was disappointing, because it leaves some questions about John and his life choices unanswered. But I understand his decision. He spent several weeks reflecting on it before delivering his final answer. Like his style of play on the basketball court, his decision-making was graceful, if a little slow. That is the sort of character his old fans would expect in our ageing hero.

The John Ritter I found and have created in this book, through memory, research, conversation, and imagination does exemplify the virtues held in head, heart, and guts that Dorothy acquired on her journey to Oz and back home. I would say to him, as an old fan from his hometown, quoting Matthew Chapter 15, "Well done good and faithful servant." Let that ideal boy, who died many years ago rest in peace. You can come home now as the man you are.

-- We still need heroes --

We have not outgrown our need for heroes. We might,

as we mature as individuals and change as a culture, want to kick the pedestal out from under our previous idols and dash them to the ground. Yet, the recent trend of expanding the term to cover victim-survivors and all law enforcement and military personnel suggests an even greater need to recognize and claim heroes for ourselves, our communities, nation, and humanity.

The rock star and pop icon Prince died on April 21, 2016, as I was working on final revisions of this book. Tributes to Prince drowned out most everything else in the media for a day or so. I heard a young Brit the night of Prince's death on NPR's broadcast of BBC Radio describe how he had marked every major event and crossroads in his life with one of Prince's songs. "You're not supposed to meet your hero, but I did," he told the reporter. The young chap had blogged about the influence Prince's music had on his life. Out of the blue Prince called him and they chatted on the phone for an hour. For this young Englishman it was as if he'd been touched by a god.

As Joseph Campbell, Sigmund Freud, Carl Jung, and other scholars and sages have shown, the Hero fulfills a psychic need for individuals and a cultural need of communities. Heroes are needed to push us and pull us toward our better selves and stronger communities -- we need our heroes to serve as guides who point us in the right way.

When a hero is no longer needed, he will likely be forgotten. Because I have come to feel for John Ritter, I risk descending into sentimentality as we come to the end of this journey. But I do not think John should be forgotten or ignored any longer in his hometown. I hope the community leaders of Goshen will act with wisdom, courage, and compassion and recognize that John Ritter still has value to offer us as a local hero. And, I hope John will accept the honors that are due him. John Ritter has made a hero's journey, and I would love to be there to see him welcomed back home in Goshen, Indiana.

I had hoped this book might be the elixir John could carry home, whether home is with his family, his current friends and employment at Circle City Tickets in Indianapolis, or back in Goshen. But that was hubris on my part. The wisdom John Ritter has gained is his. It's for him to decide with whom and when he shares the elixir he found on his journey.

About the Author

This is Jeff Rasley's ninth book. He is the author of over 50 published articles. Rasley practiced law for thirty years in Indianapolis, Indiana and was admitted to the U.S. Supreme Court Bar. He is a graduate of the University of Chicago, Indiana University School of Law, and Christian Theological Seminary. Rasley is president of the Basa Village Foundation and is liaison for the Nepal-based Himalayan expedition company Adventure GeoTreks, Ltd. He teaches a class on philosophy of philanthropy for Butler University's Honors Program. Rasley serves as an officer or director for six nonprofit organizations.

(He was an Academic All-Illinois football player at the University of Chicago.)

If you enjoyed this book, please consider other books by Jeff Rasley, such as:

- *Monsters of the Midway 1969; Sex, Drugs, Rock 'n' Roll, Viet Nam, Civil Rights, and Football*
- *Bringing Progress to Paradise: What I Got From Giving to a Village in Nepal*
- *False Prophet, a Legal Thriller*
- *Islands in My Dreams, a Memoir*
- *Pilgrimage: Sturgis to Wounded Knee and Back Home Again, a Memoir*
- *Light in the Mountains -- Namaste, Rakshi, and Electricity in a Himalayan Village*
- *India - Nepal Himalayas in the Moment*
- *Godless; Living a Valuable Life Beyond Beliefs*

Made in the USA
San Bernardino, CA
18 May 2016